Developing Leadership

Learnir
Servic

...earning and Development Manual

Peter Gilbert
and
Neil Thompson

Learning for Practice

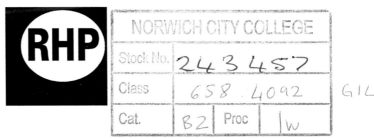

Russell House Publishing

First published in 2010 by:
Russell House Publishing Ltd.
4 St George's House
Uplyme Road
Lyme Regis
Dorset
DT7 3LS

Tel: 01297 443948
Fax: 01297 442722
e-mail: help@russellhouse.co.uk

British Library Cataloguing-in-publication Data:
A catalogue record for this book is available from the British Library.

ISBN: 978-1-905541-61-4

Editing and layout: Avenue Media Solutions, Wrexham

Printed by: Ashford Press, Bristol

About Russell House Publishing

Russell House Publishing aims to publish innovative and valuable materials to help managers, practitioners, trainers, educators and students.

Our full catalogue covers: social policy, working with young people, helping children and families, care of older people, social care, combating social exclusion, revitalising communities and working with offenders.

Full details can be found at www.russellhouse.co.uk and we are pleased to send out information to you by post. Our contact details are on this page.

We are always keen to receive feedback on publications and new ideas for future projects.

Contents

Preface

The quality of leadership is often the key difference between organisational success and failure and between an organisation being a positive, energising place to work and a negative, stressful environment.

Written by two people with a great deal of experience of both serving as leaders and offering training on the subject, this resource has a great deal to offer individuals and organisations committed to developing genuine leadership as a foundation for establishing and maintaining effective and humane workplaces.

This training manual has enabled Peter to bring together a number of themes around leadership which he has been interested in and engaged with over a number of years, in particular, an holistic approach to leadership. It links closely to, and develops, ideas presented in his book, *Leadership: Being Effective and Remaining Human* (Russell House Publishing, 2005). Neil for his part, sees leadership as a key part of promoting workplace well-being (Thompson and Bates, 2009).

Who is this manual for?

The manual will be of value in a wide range of organisations across the private, public and voluntary sectors. The authors' public service backgrounds will be apparent, and will make it especially valuable here, but this should not detract from the fact that leadership is an important issue across all organisations, regardless of sector or type.

It will be used by two main groups of people. There will be those whose duties include organising and running training courses, workshops and seminars. This could be either in-house training and development staff (training managers, staff development officers and so on, or those who provide training services on a commercial basis, whether individual freelance trainers or employees or associates of commercial training provider companies) or managers, especially senior managers (that is, managers who supervise other managers) who will be able to use the resources here to run team development sessions on the theme of leadership development.

Either group will find it invaluable in their work, both in developing the skills of actual and aspiring leaders, and in helping others learn how to train and support leaders. So it is relevant to all of these people:

- team leaders or team managers or others involved in supervising and leading groups of staff (section heads, for example);

- senior managers, both operational and strategic;

- staff in personnel or human resources sections who are responsible for advising others on matters relating to leadership ; and

- councillors, trustees, directors and others involved in policy development, implementation and review.

An earlier version of this manual was previously published as part of a training pack on supervision and leadership published by Learning Curve Publishing. It has been extensively revised and updated.

Series Editor's Foreword

About the *Learning for Practice* series

Education and training are essential underpinnings of high-quality professional practice. This series of learning and development manuals is therefore intended to provide foundations for promoting learning across the helping professions. Each manual offers guidance for new and experienced trainers alike, for managers and supervisors interested in promoting learning within their team or area of responsibility and for college or university lecturers wanting to go beyond simply delivering lectures.

The series has grown out of the Russell House *Theory into Practice* series of books which has been so successful in providing clear, short introductions to particular areas of theory as they apply to practice. Some of the manuals in this series are based on the issues covered in one or more of the books in that series, while other manuals have no direct connection with the series – although they all share a commitment to making an understanding of theory and professional knowledge more broadly accessible for practitioners and managers in order to try and make sure that our practice is *informed* practice.

The authors contributing to the series have a wealth of experience and expertise in promoting learning. Each manual therefore offers important insights, ideas and guidance that should be of great benefit in delivering high-quality learning and development events.

Experienced trainers, tutors and managers used to acting as learning facilitators should find the materials presented and the guidance given relatively straightforward. People with relatively little experience of running learning events will find the materials and guidance helpful, but may need additional support to translate the ideas given into successful learning outcomes. Such support may involve the backing of a more experienced colleague or the use of books and manuals specifically about running successful learning events, or indeed a combination of the two. So, whether experienced or not, this manual should offer a firm foundation on which to build.

About this manual

In recent years we have seen a significant shift in the direction of what has come to be known as 'managerialism', with its emphasis on targets and the inevitable bureaucracy that comes with it. But we have also seen a backlash against managerialism. Part of this has been a renewed emphasis on such important issues as spirituality, critically reflective practice and workplace well-being. Also part of this backlash can be seen as a renewed emphasis on leadership. This is because leadership is concerned with getting the best out of people, creating cultures and working environments that motivate and inspire people because they are genuinely supportive of staff and appreciative of their efforts – rather than simply trying to squeeze as much out of people as possible, which of course is counterproductive because of its negative impact on morale and its tendency to produce disaffection and stress rather than energy and commitment.

This manual has been written to support the efforts currently being made to replace mis-guided managerialist approaches to the workplace with more enlightened approaches based on principles of leadership. Written by two people with a great deal of experience of both serving as leaders and offering training on the subject, this resource has a great deal to offer individuals and organisations committed to developing genuine leadership as a foundation for establishing and maintaining effective and humane workplaces.

Neil Thompson, series editor

The series editor

Neil Thompson is a Director of Avenue Consulting Ltd, a company offering training and consultancy across the 'people professions' – that is, the helping professions plus management, supervision and leadership more broadly (www.avenueconsulting.co.uk). He has held full or honorary professorial positions at four UK universities and is now a sought-after trainer, consultant and conference speaker.

Neil has qualifications in social work; training and development; mediation and alternative dispute resolution; and management (MBA) as well as a first-class honours degree and a PhD. He is a Fellow of the Chartered Institute of Personnel and Development, the Higher Education Academy and the Royal Society of Arts, as well as a Life Fellow of the Institute of Welsh Affairs. In addition, he is a member of the International Work Group on Death, Dying and Bereavement.

Neil is a highly respected author, with over 100 publications to his name, including several bestselling books. He is the editor of the US-based international journal, *Illness, Crisis & Loss* and also edits the e-zine, *Well-being* (www.well-being.org.uk). He has been a speaker at conferences and seminars in the UK, Ireland, Spain, Italy, the Netherlands, the Czech Republic, Norway, Greece, India, Hong Kong, Canada, the United States and Australia. He is the series editor for the Russell House *Theory into Practice* series of books. His website is at www.neilthompson.info. He is also the editor-in-chief of two online communities, ***Well-being*** Zone (www.well-beingzone.com) and ***Social Work*** Focus (www.socialworkfocus.com). He has a blog on each of these sites.

Prospective authors wishing to make a contribution to the *Learning for Practice* series should contact Neil via his company website, www.avenueconsulting.co.uk.

The authors

Peter Gilbert, the author of *Leadership: Being Effective and Remaining Human* (Russell House Publishing, 2005), is an independent consultant in social and health care, currently carrying out a number of roles, including facilitating the National Social Care Strategic Network; and is also Professor of Social Work and Spirituality at Staffordshire University. Peter's other roles include being the National Project Lead for the National Forum; Chair of the National Development Team for Inclusion; and visiting Professor with Birmingham and Solihull Mental Health Foundation Trust and the University of Worcester. He also acts as an expert witness and has contributed to a number of national policy guidelines.

Following a first career in the British Army, Peter worked for 27 years in local government social services, as a practitioner/manager and senior manager. Stints with West Sussex, the London Borough of Merton and Kent Councils then saw Peter move to Staffordshire County Council as Operations Director in 1992, to take responsibility for implementing the NHS and Community Care Act 1990. He then took on the role of Director of Social Services in Worcestershire from 1997 to 2001, following local government reorganisation.

A Master's Degree in Modern History from Balliol College, Oxford, was complemented by a Master's Degree in Social Work from Sussex University, and later an MBA from Roffey Park Management Institute/Sussex University.

In addition to being the author of a book on leadership (*Leadership: Being Effective and Remaining Human*, Russell House Publishing, 2005) Peter is co-editor of *Spirituality, Values and Mental Health*, published in 2007. He recently co-authored a national position paper for SCIE on leadership and personalisation.

Neil Thompson has been involved in providing leadership training for many years as well as acting as a consultant in helping organisations to develop the necessary leadership skills to promote workplace well-being. His experience has taught him that the quality of leadership is often the key difference between organisational success and failure and between an organisation being a positive, energising place to work and a negative, stressful environment.

Neil Thompson and Peter Gilbert are also the authors of a companion volume in the *Learning for Practice* series, *Supervision Skills,* (Russell House Publishing, 2010).

Introduction

How to use this manual

Effective staff development and leadership pay dividends for all concerned in terms of:

- Higher standards of work;
- Higher levels of job satisfaction;
- A better working environment or 'climate';
- Fewer mistakes or difficult situations to deal with;
- Clearer procedures and expectations; and
- More and better opportunities for learning.

This manual can therefore play an important role in helping you develop your knowledge and skills in promoting staff development in relation to leadership.

This manual has three purposes;

i) to introduce you to what is involved in the art of leadership;

ii) to provide materials on which to base training courses and staff development exercises (for example, as part of team development work); and

iii) to act as a reference source that you can consult as and when required in the future. We therefore suggest that you read through it quite quickly the first time, to get an overview of the issues and to begin to familiarise yourself with what is involved in it. Next you should work your way slowly and thoroughly through the manual, step by step, making sure you have got to grips with each section before moving on to the next one. In this way you will steadily develop a solid foundation of understanding on which to base your work relating to developing the role of leader.

Once you have completed this second, more demanding reading of the manual, your work is still not over! You will still need to refer back to the manual from time to time (perhaps quite frequently at first until you get used to using it) as a point of reference. This, it should be added, is why – in the photocopying permission section, which follows – trainers using this manual in more than one organisation are encoraged to provide a copy of this manual to each organisation where they train.

The manual is divided into three main parts. Following this introductory section, Part One is entitled 'Setting the context', and that is precisely what it sets out to do. It discusses the importance of staff development in general before broadening out to look at what is involved in leadership and how it can be developed in a wide variety of organisations.

Part Two is entitled 'Training and Development' and, within it, you will find various exercises that can be used as the basis of training sessions or staff development activities (for example, as part of staff meetings or 'awaydays'). The exercises are clearly laid out, with guidelines for how they can be used. While inexperienced trainers are likely to feel most comfortable following the guidelines very closely, more experienced trainers may well prefer to adapt and amend as they see fit.

Part Three is the conclusion and here you will find a summary of the main themes underpinning the manual, together with suggestions for further reading, details of relevant organisations and relevant Internet resources, as well as the Appendix, which contains a set of leadership bographies and presentation slides.

Disclaimer

This manual has been researched, prepared and presented in good faith, with all due care and attention. However, no responsibility can be taken for any errors or oversights.

The manual and its contents are intended as a resource to facilitate training and staff development and should not be seen as a definitive statement of employment law. The manual is not a substitute for professional legal advice or guidance and should not be relied upon as such.

Photocopying permission for the use of the worksheets, biographies and presentation slides

1. Permission to photocopy the worksheets, biographies and presentation slides is only given to **individuals or organisations who have bought a copy of the manual** and then only for distribution at the local level within their organisation. The price of this manual has deliberately been kept affordable to smaller organisations. It is therefore expected that, as a matter of honour, larger organisations – for example, national or county-wide statutory or voluntary organisations – who might want to use the photocopiable material in numerous locations, will buy a copy of the manual for use in each locality where they are using the material.

2. If a **trainer or an educational organisation** wants to copy and distribute these worksheets, biographies and presentation slides to assist their work with clients in organisations where they are training: (a) permission is given for incidental/partial use (b) but if they want to use all or a significant part of the programme, it is expected that they will buy a copy of the book for each organisation where they undertake such training and – in line with the principles set out in point 1 (above) – a copy for each locality when they are training in a large organisation at multiple locations. This expectation is based on respect for the author's copyright and the view that providing manuals in this way will add to the benefits delivered in the training. The publisher and authors therefore seek trainers' active support in this matter.

3. Under no circumstances should anyone sell photocopied material from this manual without the express permission of the publisher.

If in doubt, anyone wanting to make photocopies should contact the publisher, via email at: help@russellhouse.co.uk.

Other photocopying permissions

Anyone wishing to copy all or part of the worksheets, biographies and presentation slides *in any context other than set out here* should first seek permission in the usual way:

- either via Russell House Publishing
- or via the Copyright Licensing Agency. (see page ii)

Anyone wishing to copy any other part of this manual in any context, beyond normal fair trading guidelines, should first seek permission in the usual way:

- either via Russell House Publishing
- or via the Copyright Licensing Agency. (see page ii)

Electronic supply of the worksheets, biographies and presentation slides

A PDF and Powerpoint of the pages of this manual, on which the worksheets, biographies and presentation slides appear, is available free, by email from RHP, to purchasers of the book who complete and return the licence request at the end of the manual.

Please note that anyone who is reading this in a copy of the manual from which the tear-out coupon has been removed would need to buy a new copy of the manual in order to be able to apply for the electronic materials.

The following terms and conditions for use of the electronic materials apply in all cases:

Terms and conditions for use of the worksheets, biographies and presentation slides from *Developing Leadership*

1. Buying a copy of *Developing Leadership* and completing the form at the back of this manual gives the individual who signs the form permission to use the materials in the PDF and Powerpoint that will be sent from RHP for their own use only.

2. The hard copies that they then print from the PDF and Powerpoint are subject to the same permissions and restrictions that are set out in the 'photocopying permission' section at the front of this manual.

3. Under no circumstances should they forward or copy the electronic materials to anyone else.

4. If the person who signs this form wants a licence to be granted for wider use of the electronic materials within their organisation, network or client base, they must make a request directly to RHP fully detailing the proposed use. All requests will be reviewed on their own merits.

- If the request is made when submitting this form to RHP, the request should be made in writing and should accompany this form.

• If the request is made later, it should be made in an email sent to help@russellhouse.co.uk, and should not only fully detail the proposed use, but also give the details of the person whose name and contact details were on the original application form.

RHP and the authors expect this honour system to be followed respectfully, by individuals and organisations whom we in turn respect. RHP will act to protect authors' copyright if they become aware of it being infringed.

Part One

Setting the Context

Reflections on leadership

It is not good enough just to preach the doctrine you have to live the life

Victoria Woodhull, US presidential candidate, 1872 (Gilbert, 2005, p.3)

An American businesswoman once remarked to one of the present authors that she heard a great deal of talk about strategy in her corporation but saw little evidence of it in practice! Leadership is another concept, like strategy, that is much bandied about but often misunderstood. The word 'leadership' is often associated with:

- 'world leaders' – presidents and prime ministers who are dubbed 'the leader' because of their role, not necessarily because of leadership qualities which they display; or
- the 'death or glory' hero depicted in Hollywood films and played by Clint Eastwood or Bruce Willis – talking tough and chewing on a cigar!

The word is tinged with macho and blockbuster connotations, and yet we also use it to describe people we read about in the papers, those we work with, or even children we observe .You often hear a remark by an adult in a school playground, concerning a child that: 'he or she is a natural leader'. With such a wide-ranging use one commentator has argued that:

Leadership is an elusive concept. Like many complex ideas, it is deceptively easy to use in everyday conversation. We may say that someone is a great leader or used great leadership in a particular situation, and others seem to understand what we mean. Nevertheless, it has proved very difficult to arrive at a precise and agreed definition of leadership. (Wright, 1996, p.6)

Yet, just as we may say about a painting: 'I don't know much about art but I know what I like', we can probably also say: 'I can't theorise about leadership, but I can recognise a leader when I meet one, and I can point out the way they are and the things they do which makes them a leader in my eyes'. (See also Goffee and Jones, 2005; Alban-Metcalfe and Alimo-Metcalfe, 2009)

One of the main thrusts for writing this training resource is to propose that leadership is a necessary component in all organisations, and both found and required at all levels. For individuals, families, groups, neighbourhoods, communities, clubs, public/private/ voluntary organisations, and countries to make progress, leadership is essential. (see Van Zwanenberg, 2010).

As George Eliot wrote in Middlemarch, about her heroine, Dorothea:

Certainly those determining acts of her life were not ideally beautiful. They were the mixed results of young and noble impulse struggling amidst the conditions of an imperfect social state, in which great feelings will often take the aspect of error, and great faith the aspect of illusion. For there is no creature whose inward being is so strong that it is not greatly determined by what lies outside it. ... Her finely touched spirits had still its fine issues, though they were not widely visible. Her full nature, like that river of which Cyrus broke the strength, spent itself in channels which had no great name on the earth. But the effect of her being on those around her was incalculably diffusive, for the growing good of the world is partly dependent on unhistoric acts, and that things are not so ill with you and me as they might have been is half owing to the number who lived faithfully a hidden life and rest in unvisited tombs. (Eliot, 1872, p. 811)

Dorothea did nothing famous but she was a force for good in the lives of those around her.

When one of the present authors (Peter) was in the Army, he had the good fortune to work with Captain, later General, Sir John Wilsey, now retired as commander of UK Land Forces, but the army inculcated leadership at all levels in the organisation by using small teams to ensure that everybody played a leadership role. In the different field of social work, Peter's first placement had an outstanding leader, Bridget Ogden, as area director. She was someone who combined a deep knowledge of practice with an ability to instil high standards in those she managed. At the next level down the team leader, Jean, was constantly motivating her team to push for higher standards and develop community initiatives as well as sound casework. At the practitioner level, Bob, was a constant source of leadership in terms of a role model, sound advice and support. (see Gilbert, 2005, Case Study 1, p. 7)

We are all likely to have our own examples from around us, but it may also be helpful to consider some major current or historical figures, for example:

Nelson Mandela, in the field of world statespeople, who opposed the apartheid regime in South Africa, was imprisoned for his beliefs, released in 1990, and was voted in as his country's first black president. Mandela wrote about his experiences in *The Long Walk To Freedom*, when he said:

I was not born with a hunger to be free. I was born free – free in every way that I could know. ... It was only when I began to learn that my boyhood freedom was an illusion, when I discovered as a young man that my freedom had already been taken from me, that I began to hunger for it. At first, as a student, I wanted freedom only for myself. ... But then I slowly saw that not only was I not free, that my brothers and sisters were not free. I saw that it was not just my freedom that was curtailed, but the freedom of everyone who looked like I did. ... That is when ... the hunger for my own freedom became the greater hunger for the freedom of my people. ... I am no more virtuous or self–sacrificing than the next man, but I found that I could not even enjoy the poor and limited freedoms I was allowed when I knew my people were not free. Freedom is indivisible; and the chains on any one of my people were the chains on all of them, the chains on all of my people were the chains on me. (Mandela, 1994, pp. 16-17)

Mandela's obvious qualities are:

• His integrity in holding firm to his beliefs; in willingness to sacrifice his personal happiness and comfort; and the forgiveness shown to his captors and political opponents.

• The formation and articulation of the vision for a new multiracial South Africa. His political opponent, ex-president de Klerk, said of Mandela:

> The ordinary man would get to the top of the hill and sit down to admire the view. For Mandela there is always another peak to climb and another one after that. For the man of destiny the journey is never complete. (quoted in Gilbert, 2005, p. 62)

• The energy to take on the presidential role in his 70s and to tour other countries on behalf of South Africa.

• His ability to live the vision – for example, wearing the Springbok rugby jersey, with its Afrikaner connotations at the final of the Rugby World Cup, held in South Africa, and the mutual embrace with Francois Pienaar, the Afrikaner Captain of the team.

This and eleven further examples are featured in the appendix at the end of this manual.

What is leadership?

> Leadership is a priceless gift which you earn from the people who work with you and you have constantly to earn that right.
> (Sir John Harvey-Jones, former Chair of ICI, 1988, p. 27)

To understand the meaning of a word it is sometimes important to return to its roots. we spoke of 'strategy' at the beginning of this part. The word is from the ancient Greek 'strategia' – generalship, and relates to an overarching plan of campaign in politics, business, war and so on. Many organisations confuse strategy with 'tactics' which are the day-to-day manoeuvres to deal with immediate circumstances.

The word 'leadership' is derived from the old English word, 'Laedan': a road, a way, the path of a ship at sea, and is related to another old English word 'Lithan' – 'to travel'. So, a leader is a person who discovers the right direction in which to travel; takes other people with them; guides them and supports them on the journey; and keeps the goal always in their mind's eye (see Gilbert and Scragg, 1992; Adair, 2002).

'Management' stems from two words: Latin noun 'manus' – a hand – and its derivative, the Italian verb 'maneggiare' – to handle or train. It epitomises control but also a 'hands on' coaching to increase skills and produce from something or someone with raw talent a controlled source of power and skill. Leadership, then, quite simply has a more dynamic ethos than 'management', with leadership's connotations of a vision of a better future, adventure, exploration and pilgrimage. The two go hand in hand, as we shall see in the next section. But leadership adds value to management and takes it on further, in the same way that management is much more than simply good administration. The review of the needs of a modern NHS, undertaken by Lord Darzi stated clearly that:

> Leadership has been the neglected element of the reforms of recent years. That must now change. (Department of Health, 2008, p.8).

The cross-departmental report *Putting People First*, made the point that leadership was an essential element if system-wide transformation was to happen (Department of Health, 2007).

As suggested in the concept of the leader as pathfinder, the ability to keep the aim of the organisation and the goals of particular tasks in mind is crucial. As it is rare that anybody can accomplish the whole task by him- or herself, the creation of the right team and their motivation is essential, especially as an enterprise expands. Also, as the strength of the team is often only as strong as its weakest link, then the leader must encourage, support and develop each individual in the team. As it has been pointed out by one commentator:

> Admittedly, there is a common theme which runs through most definitions of leadership. Most include the notion that leadership involves influence in one form or another (Yukl, 1994) .... What leaders do is to influence the behaviour, beliefs and feelings of other group members in an intended direction. (Wright and Taylor, 1994, p. 113)

John Adair (1983) in his work with the Industrial Society, produced a useful model of what he called Action-Centred Leadership (see slides 8-11).

It is reassuring that there is nothing magical about this model or the actions contained within it. We can easily be pressured into thinking that we cannot lead unless we are a Joan of Arc, Nelson Mandela, Richard Branson or General MacArthur, but the 'great leaders' may have faults as large as their virtues. Many high-profile leaders are better at building the engine of an organisation then driving it; others drive for long periods and then step down from the cab having failed to develop any successor, so as to ensure that the engine continues along the chosen path.

Max Hastings, in his book on the war of the east during World War II, considers General Douglas MacArthur in the context of the 'man of destiny' view of history. (Hastings, 2008) MacArthur was recognised as someone of considerable intellect and inspirational leadership, but he seemed bent upon 'becoming the lone star of America's Pacific war'. Hastings makes a number of pertinent comments about MacArthur's leadership style:

> MacArthur displayed a taste for fantasy quite unsuited to a field commander, together with ambition close to megalomania and consistently poor judgement in choosing subordinates... He made no jokes and possessed no small talk, though he would occasionally talk baseball to enlisted men, 'in attempts to deceive them that he was human'. Marshall (General Marshall) observed that MacArthur had 'a court', not a staff
>
> (Hastings, 2008, pp. 20-23).

This criticism links closely with Jim Collins' research into North American companies, which is suspicious of untrammelled idiosyncratic leadership (Collins, 2009).

The vision of the 'charismatic leader', if not centred on some basic values, such as respect for other human beings, can become a nightmare for those around them. Napoleon Bonaparte – still a hero in France – put in place long-standing reforms of French governance, which are still in place and effective today. His obsession with conquest, however, not only ended in France's defeat in 1815, but also a number of historians, such as Michael Roberts, have placed on Napoleon's shoulders the blame for the subsequent rise of both German militarism and the advent of communism.

Harold Geneen, legendary chief executive of the ITT company was credited with building up the strength of that organisation in a spectacular fashion. His extreme control over every facet of the organisation, and his management style, created a vacuum after his departure which led to a rapid fall from grace of the company he had built up.

The research by Sydney Finkelstein (2004) and Jim Collins (2009) demonstrates the importance of an approach which builds leaders at all levels of an organisation. Goffee and Jones (2006) remark that:

> When we ask CEO's what is their biggest problem they face, they unerringly reply: "our organisations need more leaders at every level (p. 9).

Some Conservative Party commentators, with an historical perspective, have queried whether Margaret Thatcher partially caused the election defeats for the party in 1997 and 2001, through a centralising of power in Whitehall, and a withering of the Conservative Party's grass roots in the country at large (see Blake 1997, Jenkins, 1995).

One of the main dangers for individual leaders and organisations as a whole occurs when they reach an apparent peak, and atrophy and complacency set in.

If we accept that leadership is guiding people along a path then, if like Alexander the Great you reach a point, at the end of the known world, when your troops mutiny, and you subsequently die without having developed a structure to nurture your achievements, then perhaps the result is failure, albeit in some terms a glorious one. In like fashion, the new industrial or commercial organisation, the cancer unit, the school, the football club which declines sharply when the founder or the high-profile leader departs may have been built on sand.

Sometimes the wisdom of the ancients may be a useful guide. The Chinese philosopher, Lao Tzu, writing in the 6th century BC set out his views thus:

> The best of all the leaders is the one who helps people, so that, eventually, they don't need him [or her].
> Then comes the one they love and admire.
> Next comes the one they fear.
> The worst is the one who lets people push him around.
> When there is a lack of trust people will act in bad faith.
> The best leader talks little, but what he says carry's weight.

When his work is completed and his aim fulfilled, the people will say: 'we did it ourselves'.
(Modern translation, Wilhelm, 1985. Quoted in Adair, 1983, p. 106)

Leadership integrated to practice

They can because they think they can

Virgil (670 BC)

The 1980s and 1990s in the UK saw a very strong dichotomy between attitudes towards professional practice and management. Professionals felt that being a proficient engineer, lawyer, doctor, accountant, politician, care worker, therapist, clergyperson and so on was sufficient unto itself and they didn't need to consider the bigger picture.

Handy (1978) introduced the image of the network organisation of loosely grouped professionals: the 'existential cultural type' of organisation ('Dionysus' as the particular 'god of management' in Handy's typology) has its strength in high standards in an area of expertise, and its weakness in an undeveloped sense of corporate identity and shared goals. GPs in Britain are a good example of the network organisation. In such a situation a loosely bound practice may benefit individual patients, but fail to effect positive changes in the local health economy as perhaps accomplished by a neighbouring practice which operates to a common set of objectives.

Managers believed that they had a mission to sort out 'undisciplined and hopelessly individualistic professionals'. Management's problem is that, in a world where 'knowledge', however defined, is perceived as increasingly important, expertise is personalised. As Scott (2000, p. 6) rightly points out, knowledge: 'tends to walk out of the building each night!' Kate Skinner (2010, p. 44) states that 'intellectual capital is the life blood of modern post-industrial organisations. In fact, there need to be both mutual respect between practitioners and managers and also some permeability between the two roles. While there are some dangers inherent in holding on to professional issues (see below), there is a lot to be said for having an insight into, and empathy with, 'the business' and those who carry it out 'at the sharp end'. The Greek general and writer, Xenophon, believed that there was small risk of a leader being 'regarded with contempt ... If, whatever he {sic} may have to preach, he shows himself best able to perform' (quoted in Gilbert and Scragg, 1992, p. 113). For those at the front line who fear that a move into management will be 'selling out' it is worth considering the attributes that need to be constant across both roles. It is to these that we now turn.

Personal values

To survive and prosper everybody needs a bedrock of self-belief and/or a belief in something greater than the individual. Of course, this may be a very individualistic sense of self-confidence and perhaps a driving ambition to be a highly proficient practitioner or manager, or to gain a particular position. We all have to interrelate with other people, however, and if there is an absence of integrity and a surfeit of personal ambition, that will be evident and will tend to undermine working relationships which are based considerably on trust. Most of us will have come across in our working lives 'the person who trusts nobody, and nobody trusts'. That kind of person, in the end, damages the organisation they work for and ultimately themselves. As Covey (1992) argues in his book on principle-centred leadership, personal integrity is at the core of being an effective leader. (see also Aris and Gilbert, 2007; Gilbert 2009a).

In his fascinating study of leadership issues in Shakespeare's plays, Corrigan (1999) quotes Macbeth musing: 'To know my deed 'twere best not to know myself' (p. 116). So, the tyrant has cut himself off from his own value system, so that: 'The portrayal of ambition here is like a malignant growth in Macbeth, once it has touched him it eventually takes him over. There are similar experiences in modern organisations' (p. 116).

Lack of mutual confidence can undermine even the most confident personalities. During World War Two Field Marshal Rommel, the German general most respected by the British, began to lose his sparkle, drive and even his immense tactical acumen, because of waves of mistrust emanating from the 'Men in Grey Suits' at HQ. As his biographer points out:

> Professionally, Rommel was deeply unhappy. It seemed to him that his opinion on military essentials had recently been disregarded and overruled. He felt he was no longer trusted. (Fraser, 1994, p. 404)

Level	*Principle*
Organisational	Alignment
Managerial	Empowerment
Interpersonal	Trust
Personal	Trustworthiness

(Covey, 1992) Figure 1: Four levels of principle-centred leadership, with key principles

The NHS Confederation's document on *The Challenges of Leadership in the NHS* (2007) , Zoe Van Zwanenberg's work on social care, and writings from the world of business and commerce, all stress the need for personal integrity; values espoused and lived; an authentic presence; and a distinctive voice of the leader which encourages others to show leadership in the transformation of the organisation (NHS Confederation, 2007, Van Zwanenberg, 2010, Covey, 2004). As Goffee and Jones point out, nobody wants to be led by a robotic leader, or to feel that one is being 'worked' (p. 3). As modern life and organisations increasingly demonstrate, leaders often have to work, in Julia Middleton's words: 'beyond authority', using influence and persuasion rather than command and control (see Middleton, 2007).

Increasingly, mindfulness is seen as a helpful way of developing self-awareness in both practice and management contexts for leading to better outcomes. Steven Hick suggests that the practice of deep listening enables us to 'become aware of our own dark side and own it as part of ourselves' (p.21). This is akin to Jim Collins' dictum that real leaders look into the mirror to apportion responsibility and lean out of the window to give praise (Hick, 2009).

Professional values

When consumers seek services from a professional they expect, and increasingly demand, certain values and standards. Some professions have written statements, setting out a code of behaviour, and increasingly these are defined by competencies which can be monitored for performance. The Hippocratic Oath in respect of the medical profession has a clear opening statement about not doing harm as a primary function of medicine. But tragedies, such as the Bristol Hospital children's heart surgery scandal (see Kennedy, 2001) have helped to undermine the public's confidence in the efficacy of the medical profession, because: children and their parents were not listened to and talked to honestly and openly; there was an absence of self-criticism among the senior doctors and a lack of openness to alternative views from the junior members of team; young lives were lost when they might have been saved had they been directed to more effective treatment centres.

Mannion *et al.* (2005) feature the Bristol Royal Infirmary and the Kennedy Report in their overview of NHS cultures. They point to the fact that the Infirmary had a 'club culture' 'which focussed excessive power and influence around a core group of senior managers' (p. 3). Kennedy highlighted a number of shifts in the culture of the NHS needed to make it more sensitive and responsive to the needs of patients. Sir Ian Kennedy was later made chair of the Healthcare Commission. Unfortunately, tragic events at Maidstone and Stafford General Hospitals in the last few years have highlighted how an overemphasis on narrow targets can blind management teams to the need to focus on the quality of care. The Healthcare Commission (2009), in its criticism of Stafford District General Hospital commented that the Trust's management board did not routinely discuss the quality of care.

Engineers will have a code for constructing sustainable bridges, power stations and so on, so that, when the Millennium Bridge in London had to be closed because it was unstable, many national newspapers carried pictures of bridges from Roman times to the present day which had been both stylish and safe! In fact it would be worth adding a fifth circle to Covey's diagram – professional values, with ethics as the key principle. The British Association of Social Workers has a code of practice (2002) with a commitment to five basic values:

- human dignity and worth;
- social justice;
- service to humanity;
- integrity; and
- competence.

Responsibilities as a manager, with clear links to practice, are set out so as to clearly interlink the two parts of practice and management.

While it is often mentioned that our perceived clashes between managers – those in 'grey suits', and clinicians – those in 'white coats', effective leadership, which listens to concerns at the front line and builds on sound public sector values to produce a clear vision of an improved future service, can overcome perceptual problems.

As people move from being leaders in a purely professional sense to becoming leaders for a whole group or organisation, then their professional skills and ethics can add value to their wider role, as long as professional codes don't become an excuse to hide behind (see below).

The potential negative side of professionalism is the elitism and arrogance inherent in the notion that: 'the professional knows best'. The creative side is offering an array of skills and possibilities that the consumer is not aware of. An obituary on the inspirational producer and broadcaster, John Walters, quoted him as stating: 'We are not here to give people what they want. We are here to give people what they didn't know they wanted' (*The Guardian,* 1 August 2001). There is a very thin dividing line between aspiration and arrogance.

In an interview, Ian McPherson, the Director of the Government's National Mental Health Development Unit, speaks of his experience of depression and being a mental health service user, and how this is vital in allowing him to 'understand what it feels like' to be seen as separate or 'that person over there with a mental illness'.(O'Hara, 2009).

The effective social or health service practitioner will move from positive listening to positive action. Egan (1986) writes:

> Helpers are seen as competent because they are active, because they
> listen intently … talk intelligently … are understanding, genuine and respectful.
> (p. 27)

In all this, Egan argues that 'helpers must be able to deliver'. These attributes are just as crucial in the industrial and commercial worlds where attentiveness to the consumer, the finance houses and all the parts of the vertical integration chain are vital.

Managing oneself

In introducing a new course in developing leadership potential at Roffey Park Management Institute in 2001, the programme director, Chris Lake, announced that the leaders we are most impressed with tend to be:

> almost without exception … people with high self-esteem, whose actions are
> congruent with their espoused views, who understand their own beliefs and
> values and who have a strong sense of their own direction. To be truly effective
> as a leader, you've got to be comfortable with who you are and what you are
> about. Essentially, concentrating on leading yourself is a powerful way to grow
> your ability to lead others.
> (quoted in Gilbert, 2005, p. 1)

Just as values and direction are vital for an organisation, so are they for each individual leader. It is very difficult for staff to follow someone who has no value compass; who doesn't appear confident in themselves; has left the map at the start of the journey; and is constantly wandering up culs-de-sac! (See also Alban-Metcalfe and Alimo-Metcalfe, 2009; Gilbert, 2009).

Thinking things through and thinking ahead

The well-motivated and orientated practitioner will be both concentrating on the job in hand and centred in their present but also looking ahead. The surgeon, the advertising copywriter, actor, salesperson, junior commander in the armed services, clergyperson and so on has to do 'a really professional job' of work in the here and now, based on their personal and professional values; but they must also look ahead to the latest research and practice, so as to challenge themselves and those around them to improve products and services.

This is at the heart of good management, effective leadership, and their combination. We shall develop this in the next section.

Leadership and management

> I keep six honest serving men
> (they taught me all I know)
> Their names are what and why and when
> And how and where and who
>
> Rudyard Kipling (1865-1936)

Context

In the 1950s most organisations in the UK were administered, not managed. The interwar years had seen a profound sense of disillusionment from the economic and social optimism of the Victorian era and the Liberal reforms of the early 20th century. The loss during the Great War of so many leaders, and often whole communities in the 'pals battalions', coupled with class conflict in the 1920s and the sense of betrayal in the perceived breach of the postwar 'social contract', bred cynicism and stagnation. The aftermath of the Second World War saw a greater sense of social cohesion and a belief in an underpinning welfare state. But it also bred complacency and the sense that the war had been the great effort, and therefore leadership need not be taken into the peacetime era. Britain was seen as a leader in 'administration': the civil service, the judiciary, colonial administration, the professions – all fields in which the UK saw itself as a world leader. But as America, western Europe and the Far East moved forward in radically different ways, Britain found itself left behind, not only in wealth creation but in social welfare as well.

Although Britain made the right decision in trying to 'win the peace' at the same time as striving to 'win the war', through the support given to the work of William Beveridge, and the development of the NHS, social insurance, national assistance and childcare, the country made the fundamental mistake of not rethinking its role in the world. The government still saw Britain as a world power and its expenditure and commitment to those aims undermined progress in other fields. Midwinter, in his excellent overview of social history in Britain claims that: 'the nation was now in the position of the [wo]man with champagne tastes and beer pockets' (1994, p. 93).

While foreign commentators praised: 'the English way of reconciling respect for liberty with a very high degree of public order and co-operation' (Martin Wiener, US academic, quoted in Midwinter, 1994, p. 106), the reforms were essentially gradualist, and where they were more radical, as in housing policy with the proliferation of high-rise ghettos, the approach was mistaken, with long-term, adverse social and economic consequences. Midwinter comments on the role of women in society: 'the welfare state improved the lot of women without *changing* it' (p. 108, emphasis added), is a constant complaint for the postwar years.

In British industry the most often quoted example is that of British Leyland, with its reputation for shoddy work – the 'Friday car', and divisive industrial relations. But, just as undermining in the long term was a failure within senior management to plan ahead a viable range of models that the public wanted to buy. With a lack of customer responsiveness in models and reliability, pleas to 'buy British' (reinforced by films such as 'The Italian Job') fell on deaf ears.

The country was alarmed to find that it seemed to have 'won the War' but 'lost the peace', both in economic terms and then in what its economy could purchase in terms of health and welfare. Technological innovation was often spectacular but undeveloped, while the institutions and professions were unreformed, with inadequate internal and external scrutiny. As Leadbeater (1999) remarks:

> We are timid and cautious where the Victorians were confident and innovative. We live within the shell of institutions the nineteenth century handed down to us. Our highly uneven capacity for innovation is the source of our unease. We are scientific and technological revolutionaries, but political and institutional conservatives. (p. x)

Sound administration came to be seen as useful but insufficient in itself, and belatedly Britain began to consider management as a way of coping with the increasing complexity of organisational change.

	Administration	Management
Objectives	Stated in general terms and reviewed or changed infrequently	Stated as broad strategic aims supported by more detailed short-term goals and targets reviewed
Success criteria	Mistake avoiding Performance rarely measurable	Success seeking Performance mostly measurable
Resource use	Secondary task	Primary task
Decision making	Has to make few decisions but affecting many and can take time over it	Has to make many affecting few and has to make them quickly

	Administration	*Management*
Structure	Roles defined in terms of areas of responsibility. Long hierarchies; limited delegation	Shorter hierarchies maximum delegation
Roles	Arbitration	Protagonist
Attitudes	Passive: workload determined outside the system. Best people used to solve problems	Active: seeking to influence the environment. Best people used to find and exploit opportunities
	Time insensitive	Time sensitive
	Risk avoiding	Risk accepting but minimising it
	Emphasis on procedure	Emphasis on results
	Doing things right	Doing the right thing
	Conformity	Local experiments: need for conformity to be proved
	Uniformity	Independence

Figure 2: The different characteristics of administration and management (Gilbert and Scragg, 1992, derived from Rees, 1984)

Sir Gerry Robinson, in his foreword to the NHS Confederation *Challenges of Leadership* document points out that: 'there is not much history of management in the NHS. It has been about administration rather than leadership. I felt that managers do not believe they have the right to manage … it probably feels safer not to do something than to stick your neck out' (2007, p. 2). In his BBC series *Can Gerry Robinson Fix the NHS?*, Robinson had some difficulty in persuading the Chief Executive that it was important for him to come out of his office and engage with the front line, so as to comprehend the patient experience; gather ideas for service improvement from those undertaking the actual work face to face and day to day; and to demonstrate to staff that he was interested in their work and their welfare. A middle manager recently commented to one of the present authors that her Director of Adult Services was: 'Professional; passionate about service delivery; challenging, yet warm; a good listener; and inspirational – a real person'. We would probably all like to work for someone like that!

Kotter (1988; 1990) has charted the changing scene for modern businesses: the heightened complexity of the business environment; the pace of change; the intricate nature of organisations and organisational relationships; and the interaction between individuals, organisations and the state. For Kotter (1988, p. 15) a 'world of intense competitive activity among very complex organisations' will be one where bureaucratic managers become not only irrelevant but dangerous, and in which even the best 'professional' managers may be ineffective unless they can also lead.

The medium-sized manufacturing company feeling inured against change by a stable market and patents on its products; the building society relying on a fixed customer –

base and a small number of product lines; the acute hospital which presumes that its local GPs will continue to refer their patients whatever the quality of service; these are all living in a world which is passing. Charles Handy's work has concentrated in large part on the effects of a changing world. One example from the past he uses is that of the indigenous peoples of South America, with their advanced civilisations, failing to recognise the threat posed by the fleet of the Spanish conquistadors, because never having seen a European sailing ship before, they thought the sails were clouds (Handy, 1989).

The 2008/09 credit crunch and subsequent recession appear to have been the result of considerable strategic blindness and lassitude by politicians and regulators. Most of the practices defied basic logic, or as Vince Cable puts it: 'hubris is giving way to nemesis' (Cable, 2009).

For many organisations today, a failure to identify a growing complexity within, or to ascertain increasing threats from without, spells the beginning of the end.

What managers do depends partly on:

- What they see their job as being.
- How they see their staff as being motivated.
- The external pressures as a whole.
- The day-to-day pressures which mean 'the urgent' pushes out the 'important'.

Carlson (1951) and Mintzberg (1973) in major research on the nature and scope of the work managers do, found their actual working day incredibly fragmented – with very little time spent in the serene, reflective creation of strategy; and a great deal spent in fire-fighting of various kinds, administrative routine and office politics (see Stewart, 1985).

As the doyen of management theory, Peter Drucker, writes:

> In fact, executives might well be defined as people who normally have no time of their own, because their time is always pre-empted by matters of importance to somebody else. (1986, p. 9) (See also Drucker with Maciarello, 2008)

However their role is defined, managers will inevitably start to shape the job in their own way. Some may consciously copy the director in Blanchard and Johnson's *One Minute Manager* (1983), who has a clear desk after his weekly goal-setting meeting. Others will be spending more time with those who work for them, because theirs is a people-inten-sive business, or the pace of change requires more personal contact; another may be devoting considerable time to working laterally with other departments within the organi-sation; another with customers; and yet another with stakeholders of different kinds, including the board, shareholders, political committees and so on.

To ensure that the manager keeps his or her eye on the goals of the organisation, they need to have methods of ensuring that these multifaceted activities, meritorious in their own right, actually contribute to a coherent whole. The basic question: 'How is what I'm doing contributing to the goals of my team/organisation?', is a good prompt to ensure that the individual is on the right track, as are Kipling's words at the beginning of an earlier section. It is easy to jump from the 'why' and the 'what' of strategic management to the more tactical tasks of 'who' is going to do something, 'how' and 'when'. Cunningham (1999), in his work on strategic learning in organisations, is clear on how central the 'why' questions are to clarifying and maintaining strategic direction. See Figure 3 below.

'Everything I have learnt', writes Sir John Harvey-Jones, 'teaches me that it is only when you work with rather than against people that achievement and lasting success is possible.' (1988, p. 7). The key word here is 'lasting'. Management practice which is oppressive and lacks integrity may provide short-term wins but is essentially limited.

Organisations as a whole, as much as individual managers, need to discover ways of motivating employees in ways which recognise a demographic shortfall of labour, a lacuna in specialist skills and a desire in the workers to have more self-fulfilment and empowerment.

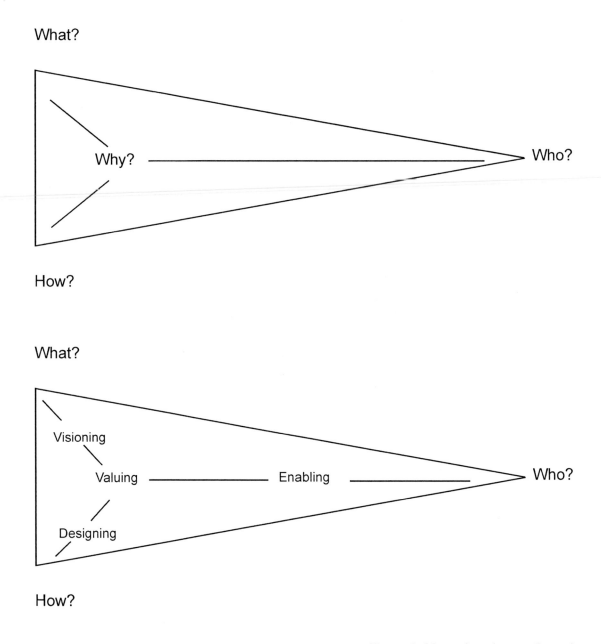

Figure 3: Managing change through leadership, Cunningham (1999)

Scott (2000) identifies 'eight waves of reinvention' from 1985 to 1999:

- quality movements;
- downsizing;
- re-engineering;
- core competencies;
- mergers and acquisitions;
- outsourcing;
- networked computing; and
- empowerment.

All these movements have achieved cost efficiencies in both private and public sectors, but with decreasing returns in terms of cost benefits, and an increasing alienation of employees. As one annual audit of employee attitudes put it:

> It is disturbing to report such an erosion of loyalty amongst internal customers (ie staff) when most firms are so validly pursuing loyalty campaigns with their external customers. (Scott, 2000, p. 8)

Executives need to be clear about how they see the factors which motivate demotivate those who work for them. It was the American social scientist, Douglas McGregor (1960) who worked up his theory X and theory Y, based on a pessimistic/optimistic or 'original sin'/perfectibility dichotomy, and that is depending on our model of humanity. In theory X people are seen as naturally lazy and needing a stick and carrot approach; in theory Y workers are seen as basically self-motivated but requiring a favourable environment in which to work. In the 1980s, Peters and Waterman (1982) and William Ouchi (1981), were instrumental in trying to puzzle out why companies in the 'Tiger Economies' of the Far East were more successful than their US and UK counterparts. Ouchi came up with Theory Z. See Figure 4 overleaf.

The seminal work of Herzberg (1960) is useful in pulling these theories together. When he interviewed workers in the United States, his survey groups identified two sets of factors: hygiene or maintenance factors, which would cause dissatisfaction if they were absent, and motivators which gave a positive incentive. The hygiene or maintenance factors were company policy, administration, supervision, interpersonal relations, status, a salary, security and the impact of the job on personal life. The motivators were achievement, recognition, responsibility, advancement, interesting work, and the possibility of personal growth.

Clearly many of these interlock and it is the responsibility of managers to look at individual and small group methods rather than the blanket approach that proved so unsuccessful as incentives in the old Soviet Union economy or the British car industry of the 1980s.

There is often very little room for manoeuvre in the public sector which has over-relied in the past on 'job satisfaction'. Here an even more imaginative approach must be used with recognition, career structures for advanced practice, opportunities for personal growth and the building of effective teams which enjoy working and possibly recreating together. The administrative burden needs to be lifted as far as possible within the

Theory X	Theory Y	Theory Z
People dislike work and try to avoid it	People see work as fulfilling part of their psychological need to find value and meaning	People identify with a corporate vision, value system & presentation which is accurate and explicit
People work only if you use a 'carrot and stick' approach	Most people can be motivated if given a realistic and noble goal to aim for	Workers respond to clear and achievable organisational goals
People avoid responsibility at all costs	Self-discipline is far more effective than that imposed from outside.	Teamwork and intensive socialisation have worked well for Japanese firms in Europe, the USA and Japan
Money and fear make things happen!	People enjoy the challenge of responsibility if given guidance and support	
People are only creative when it's a case of trying to buck the system	The desire to realise our full potential is even more powerful	Individualised performance-related pay is a motivator
	There is a great deal of untapped creativity waiting to to be released	Each individual should feel a hero/heroine in trying to improve own performance
		Creativity exists but organisations have the responsibility to ensure that knowledge and skills are made available to workers so as to translate motivation into performance.

Figure 4: Theories of individual motivation (Gilbert and Scragg, 1992, derived from McGregor, 1960, and Ouchi, 1981) (See also Scragg, 2009)

constraints of public accountability, and employees need much greater feedback that the work they are doing day by day is having a positive effect and changing people's lives. Alan Fowler, considering the issues from a public sector perspective, makes eight key points:

- How well people work is influenced as much by attitude and motivation as by competence.
- Motivation is affected by an amalgam of influences – personal, job related, environmental and managerial.
- Managers need to understand that each employee is a unique individual.
- Jobs need to be meaningful and interesting, and people need feedback on their performance.
- Work needs to be seen as partially a social process, and motivation is affected by group attitudes.
- In organisations, general culture has a strong motivational influence.
- Motivation can be stimulated by effective systems of recognition and reward.
- Managerial leadership is vital: qualities such as consistency, commitment, fairness, decisiveness and communication are common factors.

Fowler stresses that:

for managers, the requirement is to know each employee well and so understand the individual characteristics which are likely to influence each person's motivation. (1988, p. 64)

For the manager who is tempted to delude themselves that frontline workers will be fooled by facile motivators, a good corrective is to read Scott Adams' books featuring the archetypal employee, Dilbert. One of the most famous cartoons has the managing director saying:

> I've been saying for years that employees are our most valuable asset. It turns out that I was wrong. Money is our most valuable asset. Employees are ninth. (Adams, 1997, p. 53)

One of the employees replies: 'I'm afraid to ask what came in eighth?', to which the managing director responds: 'carbon paper'!

Wheatley (1999), poses the enduring questions:

> How do we create structures that are flexible and adaptive, that enable rather than constrain? How do we simplify things without losing what we value about complexity? How do we resolve personal needs for autonomy and growth with organisational needs for prediction and accountability. (p. 79)

The managerial tasks

Researchers, theorists and management practitioners (Clutterbuck and Crainer, 1990; Adair, 1983; Kotter, 1990; Hunt, 1991; Clegg *et al.* 2005;) agree that there are a clearly defined set of managerial tasks where the skills can be learned:

1. Creating the agenda

Developing a plan for future action – a map of how to achieve the objectives plus the financial resources to achieve success. This is the 'why' and the 'what', and the agenda needs to have both an overarching map and a number of specific objectives and sub-tasks to achieve it. The plan must be realistic and able to be assessed to see if it is successful. As Adair puts it:

> All leaders need this skill of quarrying objectives out of aims, and then cutting steps into the objectives so that they can be achieved. (1983, p. 79)

It is worth reflecting on Field Marshal Rommel's dictum that: 'no plan survives contact' (Fraser, 1994, p. 418). The bureaucratic manager will be at a loss when that brilliantly created plan hits practical problems from productive capacity, market demand, shareholder confidence and so on. The leader is likely to have the ability to rethink and plan anew. Peter Drucker recalls that the American president, Franklin D. Roosevelt, who masterminded the American recovery from economic recession and their success in World War Two, found that, when he became president in 1933, his plan for economic recovery was upset by changed circumstances.

> Roosevelt immediately substituted a political objective for his former economic one. He switched from recovery to reform. He knew that he had to change his plans radically to have any hope of success (Drucker, 1967, p. 129)

2. Organising and human resources

Getting the right people for the job in hand, with potential to grow in the job is essential. The American chief of staff in World War II, George Marshall, had a maxim that, if someone was not up to the task in hand they must be replaced, but that each person would almost certainly have skills which could be used productively elsewhere, and these should be ascertained and utilised. Staff have to be communicated with intensely on the aim; briefed on the objectives and tasks; listened to and worked with; and enthused.

When one of the present authors (Peter) was the Director of Operations for Staffordshire Social Services, working through both cultural and service change, he coined a simple phrase to be used in respect of users and carers, staff and stakeholders: 'Listen – Hear – Respond – Act' - a quick check, integral to the change process. In both practice and management listening needs to be active.

> MAPPING → SERVICE → VALUES → CULTURE → MISSION → VISION → PRINCIPLES
>
> Figure 5: Vision and change processes in social services (Gilbert, 2005)

Of course 'hearing' does not necessarily mean that you do what others want you to. But the more complex and unpopular the decision, the greater the need for good communication.

3. Controlling and problem solving

Managers monitor progress on the plan from a number of perspectives, remembering that shareholders and financial markets in the private sector and central government in the public sector will have their own view as to what constitutes successful adherence to the plan.

It is essential that not only the lessons of success and failures are learned (and there is the temptation either to want only the good news or, conversely, opine, like Aristotle, that people only learn from failure, never from success), but also that the learning processes themselves are studied – that is, 'double-loop learning', rather than the 'single loop' of the issue itself. (Argyris and Schön, 1974; Cunningham, 1999).

A useful checklist of the functions and tasks, set out to be congruent with Adair's model appears in the appendix of this manual.

So, where does leadership come in, and is it different from management?

> If you do not know which port you are sailing to, no wind is favourable
>
> Seneca (64BC)

At the time of a crisis, war or rapid technological, political, democratic or economic turbulence, countries and organisations of all types and sizes need people at the helm who can initiate change and lead through it – riding the white waters of change. The leader must have both a clear eye for where they want to get to on the other side of the rapids and a keen eye for the boulders coming up immediately in front of the raft. At the same time, the leader will have to encourage the crew, who may be frightened, apathetic, weary or underskilled.

Times of change are both dangerous and an opportunity, but it is easy to hit the rocks or be thrown out of the canoe. As the old master, Niccolo Machiavelli wrote:

> Nothing is more difficult to handle, more doubtful of success, and more dangerous to carry through than initiating changes in a state's constitution. The innovator makes enemies of all those who prospered under the old order, and only lukewarm support is forthcoming from those who would prosper under the new. (1981, p. 51, originally published 1514)

Machiavelli also asserts that the effective ruler will look ahead to map the possible futures, even when the waters are calm. For, as he puts it, the wise ruler not only copes with present troubles but also with ones likely to arise in the future, and assiduously forestalls them:

> When trouble is sensed well in advance it can be easily remedied; if you wait for it to show itself any medicine will be too late because the disease will have become incurable. (p. 39)

Paul Corrigan's book on Shakespeare's plays and their lessons for today's managers (Corrigan, 1999) uses *Henry the Fifth* to portray the different ways a leader has to manage through danger and trauma to reach his or her goals. Some of the decisions political and military leaders have to make most of us hope will not be a cross we have to carry but, as Corrigan writes of Henry, he took dark decisions as well as those where he is seen as a knight in shining armour: 'The greatness of the play is that leadership is not simple, but full of ambiguities' (p. 149).

As we saw earlier, leadership comes with its accent on change processes. It is a different concept from management, with its accent on control. The first produces necessary change to steer country, company, public body and so on through the rapids (to continue our white water analogy); the second ensures the sails and oars are in good condition, and the boat is well supplied with food.

Leadership is different from management, but neither is sufficient on its own. Management on its own never produces significant and necessary change; leadership, left without the anchor of good management, can lead to chaos in its wake. In a modern context both are essential for the survival and growth of the organisation. Strong management without the leadership factor can lead to stifling, bureaucratic entities producing order for order's sake. Leadership without sound management can result in being forced into change for change's sake, or pulled in a messianic and destructive direction. The best example of the latter is Hitler's Germany, a story of brilliant and diabolical mass manipulation which still haunts us today. Keegan's (1987) text in military leadership, *The Mask of Command*, demonstrates this, as does Kershaw's (1991) study of Adolf Hitler, which gives a fascinating insight into the fact that the Nazi state was far from monolithic and, in fact, was poorly managed, with a divide and rule technique. (See also Kershaw, 2009).

John P. Kotter's work on leadership is very concise and easy to follow. He sets out the relationship between leadership and management in a number of key texts (1988, 1990, 1996). A brief summary of the relationship between vision, strategies, plans and budgets is shown below:

Leadership:

- Inspires a vision – an appealing, stretching, yet practical picture of the future.
- Creates strategies – setting out how the vision can be achieved in practice.

Management:

- Produces plans – mapping out the 'hows', 'whens' and 'whos' to implement the strategies.
- Formulates budgets – plans are translated into financial projections and goals.

(see Kotter, 1996)

Theories of leadership

1. The singer not the song: charismatic leadership

Some of the first theories of leadership were around the concept of the charismatic persona (see Smith and Peterson, 1988). It is easy to see the attraction of this idea and to concentrate on some of the high-profile current and historical figures who appear to embody particular characteristics.

Keegan's (1987) study of Alexander the Great shows a man of:

- great vision;
- extraordinary energy;
- personal (in fact reckless) courage;
- excellent logistical sense;
- cultural sensitivity and inquiry;
- an ability and willingness to encourage talented subordinates;
- a demonstrative empathy with his soldiers; and
- a talent for weaving stories to reinforce his vision.

The historian, Arrian, tells us that, after a battle, Alexander:

> showed much concern about the wounded, visiting each, examining their wounds, asking how they were received, and encouraging each to recount and even boast of his exploits. (Quoted in Keegan, 1987, p. 46)

Edwards and Townsend (1965) discerned a number of qualities in successful business people:

- strength of character and willingness to work hard;
- perseverance and single mindednes;
- commercial flair;

- a willingness to take risks; and
- an ability to inspire enthusiasm.

Argyris (1953), observing American executives, drew up a list of ten characteristics, though by no means all of these would be found in each individual:

- a high tolerance of frustration;
- the ability to engage full participation from people;
- self-questioning, without self-doubt;
- an understanding of the 'laws of competitive warfare';
- the ability to express negative feelings tactfully;
- the ability to accept victory with controlled emotions;
- recovery from setbacks;
- an understanding of the need for bad news to be given;
- identification with groups; and
- realistic goal setting. (p. 53)

Peter Drucker was exceedingly sceptical about this approach. 'I soon learned,' he wrote, that there is no 'effective personality .... all they [effective executives] have in common is the ability to get the right things done' (1967, p. 18). As a footnote, he adds caustically that he knows many highly effective – and successful – executives who lack most, if not all, of Argyris's 'characteristics'. 'I also know quite a few who, though they answer to Argyris's description, are singularly ineffective!' (ibid.).

Drucker puts forward five elements of 'competency' which he believes anyone can attain and which lead to effectiveness:

- the management of time;
- a focus on results;
- an ability to build on strengths – their own and those of superiors, colleagues, subordinates and the situation overall;
- concentration on a few major areas where superior performance will produce outstanding results; and
- making effective decisions – taking the right steps in the right sequence.

The problems with the charismatic or trait theory of leadership are:

- The emphasis tends to be on the individual, not the people who have to carry out the vision and tasks, or the environment in which the organisation operates. It is too much 'I' and not enough 'we'.
- The charismatic leader, often an entrepreneur in a business sense or a states(wo)man setting up a new nation state may be excellent at starting something off, but hopeless at embedding an organisation/state which can carry the vision forward.
- Such people often don't know when to step aside, or believe themselves to be so much part of the country/company that they are irreplaceable. No successors are groomed and what is left is a lack of leadership to take over, or, in Alexander's case, too many strong leaders and the almost immediate break up of his empire. (See Collins, 2009)

• Separation from 'the followers' (citizens, employees, communities and so on) can take place, leading to disintegration. Corrigan's study of Shakespeare's Roman general 'Coriolanus' shows him as initially successful but isolating himself from all his followers. As one of his soldiers describes him: 'he is himself alone' (Coriolanus, Act 1, Scene 4). By contrast, St Benedict of Nursia, in his Rule, which has endured for many centuries in building effective communities, urged that his chief executive, the Abbot should call the whole community together when anything important was to be decided, because sometimes the most junior would have the best ideas (The Rule of St Benedict, c540AD, English version, 1982; See also Jamison, 2006). Followers are essential, as Kelley (1988) argues.

The leader who engages with and encourages good followership, and also demonstrates it him- or herself when appropriate, is likely to be hugely influential.
• The direction of the charismatic leader may be one that leads to evil outcomes as easily as good ones. As Peter Senge (1990) has pointed out, leaders: must be able to help people understand the systemic forces that shape change. It is not enough to intuitively grasp these forces. Many 'visionary strategists' have rich intuitions about the cause of change, intuitions they cannot explain. They end up being authoritarian leaders. (p. 123)

However, despite the potential problems of the charismatic leader, most of us wish to work with and for people who bring meaning to the workplace; who move us; who resonate with us (see Boyatzis and McKee, 2005). 'Resonant leaders', to use Boyatzis and McKee's phrase, are good at weaving stories which promote a common approach to overcoming obstacles and reaching new goals (see Bates and Gilbert, 2008).

2. Cometh the time, cometh the (wo)man: situational leadership

To return to Machiavelli again, the canny Florentine advises leaders to select the qualities and strategies they need to suit the situation they find themselves in. From history, he suggests that a ruler in a time of instability would wish to select qualities from the Emperor Severus (soldier and statesman) – who could be both 'lion and fox' to 'establish his state', and the attributes of Marcus Aurelius (philosopher and statesman), when skills are needed to maintain the state, 'after it has been established and made secure' (Machiavelli, 1514, p. 114).

In modern times, Robert Tannenbaum and Warren Schmidt believed that managers should consider three interrelated factors:

- their own character and qualities;
- those of their subordinates; and
- the situation at the time.

Managers' characteristics that are important in deciding how to manage include:

- their value system;
- the confidence or not they have in their subordinates;
- their leadership style; and
- their ability to cope with ambiguity.

The characteristics of their followers include:

- their dependence/independence;
- the ability to assume responsibility;
- their tolerance of uncertainty – the need to be directed or their preference for greater choice in decision- making;
- identification with the goals of the organisation; and
- experience and expertise.

The characteristics of the situation include:

- the type and culture of the organisation;
- the effectiveness of the teams;
- the scale and nature of the challenge; and
- the amount of time available to make decisions.

(Tannenbaum and Schmidt, 1958, quoted in Stewart 1985).

This was further developed by Hersey (1984) and Ken Blanchard's *One Minute Manager* series. In *Leadership and the One Minute Manager*, Blanchard *et al.*, (1986) set out four basic leadership styles to be utilised appropriately:

1. *Directing* – the leader provides specific instructions and closely supervises task accomplishment.
2. *Coaching* – the leader continues to direct and closely supervise, but also explains decisions, solicits suggestions, and supports progress.
3. *Supporting* – the leader facilitates and supports subordinates' efforts towards accomplishing the task, and shares responsibility for decision making with them.
4. *Delegating* – the leader turns over responsibility for decision making and problem solving to subordinates.

3. 'Both/and' not 'either/or'

Peters and Austin (1985) speak of a need to find a new way of inspiring people:

> for the last 25 years, we have carried around with us the image of manager as a cop, referee, devil's advocate, dispassionate analyst, professional, decision-maker ... The alternative we now propose is leader ... as cheer-leader, enthusiast, nurturer of champions, hero finder, wanderer, dramatist, coach, facilitator, builder. (p. 267)

This is a model which relates back to our earliest traditions of leadership, as a reading of Greek literature and Anglo-Saxon history and poems will demonstrate.

While the management role is sometimes referred to as 'transactional leadership' (a process of exchanges: votes for political office; salary for work; training to meet assessed needs), at times of change, there is a need to transform people and organisations and actively bear upon situations, hence, 'transformational leadership', or what Kotter (1988) calls 'the leadership factor'.

Managers:

- focus on systems and structures;
- maintain;
- ask **how** and **when**;
- concentrate on planning and budgeting;
- have their eye on the bottom line;
- are deductive and rational;
- ensure the accomplishment of plans by controlling and problem-solving;
- cope with current complexity; and
- do things right.

Leaders:

- focus on people;
- develop;
- ask **what** and **why**;
- set a direction and align people;
- have their eyes on the horizon;
- are inductive and intuitive;
- achieve goals through motivating and inspiring people;
- cope with change; and
- do the right thing.

Figure 6: Leadership and management compared, Kotter (1988)

It was James McGregor Burns who initially spelled out the radical difference between the two:

> Transforming leadership, while more complex than transactional leadership, is more potent. The transforming leader recognises an existing need or demand of a potential follower. But, beyond that, the transforming leader looks for potential motives in followers, seeks to satisfy higher needs, and engages the full person of the follower. (1978, p. 92)

As we have said, both management (transactional) and leadership (transformational) need to be in place for an organisation to prosper in a variety of situations.

As success for banks, hospitals, hotels, airline companies, political parties, sales centres and so on increasingly depends on each and every person in the chain of production and supply working at their very best, leadership, management and followership skills are required at every level.

Finkelstein's work (2004) points to the fact that leaders who are successful for a particular cycle for the organisation's life, may not learn sufficient lessons to take the organisation forward, and may in a sense be victims of their own success. Jim Collins' latest work (Collins, 2009) charts a number of international companies which began their fall from grace with a stage one which Collins terms: 'hubris (the Greek for the kind of pride that precedes a fall) borne of success' and moves on to the 'undisciplined pursuit of more'; 'denial of risk and peril'; 'grasping for salvation'; and, finally – 'capitulation to irrelevance or death'.

Collins also warns that 'a culture of bureaucratic mediocrity can gradually replace a culture of disciplined excellence' (p. 56). This is particularly relevant for public sector organisations which can sometimes turn bureaucracy into an art form. A review of UK defence spending, published in October 2009 stated 'that the system is failing to procure the equipment we **don't** need (emphasis added). The report on the crash of an RAF Nimrod plane in Afghanistan in 2006, killing 14 personnel, was investigated by Charles Haddon-Cave QC. He declared that the MoD's safety system was not fit for purpose. The provider failed to deliver a safe system and the Ministry, as commissioner and consumer failed to check it was getting the right product. Haddon-Cave criticised an organisational culture which 'has allowed business priorities' to overcome concentrating on airworthiness (Haddon-Cave, 2009).

Bass and Avolio (1994) have taken Kotter's leadership tasks further and linked them with an inspirational approach, which they refer to as the Four 'I' approach:

1.   *Idealised influence* – Transformational leaders behave in ways that result in their being role models for their followers. The leader shares risks with subordinates and is consistent rather than arbitrary.

2.   *Inspirational motivation* – the leader motivates and inspires, and creates clearly communicated expectations that people wish to meet.

3.   *Intellectual stimulation* – the stimulation of innovation and creativity is important. Staff are encouraged to try new approaches – for example, Kemal Attaturk, the creator of the Turkish state, well-known for somebody who, even in private life, would always be encouraging of the people around him to raise difficult questions and try to answer them.

4.   *Individualised consideration* – Transformational leaders pay special attention to each individual's needs for achievement and growth.

To ensure that the transformational approach is not just an end in itself – an organisational 'feel-good factor', Nicholls (1999) has added a third stage:

> Value-centred leadership – directing the energy within transformational leadership towards the fundamental purpose of creating and delivering value to the customer, patient, citizen and so on – thus creating strategic leadership, that moves forward the transactional functions of management and the transforming powers of leadership, with a depth of purpose and extended vision for the future. (p. 17)

> • *Stage 1: Managerial leadership*: Two components: supervsiory (hands) and strategic (head). Important in going beyond mere administration.
>
> • *Stage 2: Transforming leadership:* Inspirational leadership (heart) is added to hands and head. This engages people in a vision and gives them 'headroom' to perform.
>
> • *Stage 3: Value-centred leadership:* 'Managers with positive Values, apply Transforming Leadership to the fundamental business purpose of creating and delivering Value to the Customer'
>
> Figure 6: Moving to a higher management level (derived from Nicholls, 1999)

As the former President of South Africa, F.W. de Klerk, said of his successor:

> Mr Mandela has walked a long road and now stands at the top of the hill. A traveller would sit down to an admire the view, but the man of destiny knows that beyond this hill lies another and another – the journey is never complete. (quoted in Gilbert, 2005, p. 62)

Creating an effective culture

To ensure the delivery of the outcomes the organisation requires, managers must be able to check that they have engaged with all the different elements relevant to the organisation – both externally and internally. A useful model is the Seven 'S' approach of McKinsey, as discussed in Peters and Waterman (1982) and Hampden-Turner (1990). The model has the following elements:

Have a clear set of SHARED VALUES
Develop the STRATEGY
Hire the right STAFF
Train them in the relevant SKILLS
Manage them in an appropriate STYLE
Install the correct SYSTEMS
Shape a STRUCTURE to perform the function.

At the heart of the model, however, has to be some key elements which are essential if the whole process is not to become soulless and sterile. These elements are:

• *Leadership* – a desire and ability to be a pathfinder for the organisation.
• *Shared values* – fundamental beliefs about the way we act in the world, and that are held in common.
• *Core goals* – which are at the epicentre of the strategy.
• *A positive culture* – which gives congruent messages about the company and its people through a variety of mediums, and is ultimately tested by the experience of the customer and stakeholders. (See Gilbert, 2005, p.30)

What is culture?

Edgar Schein, a leading figure in the study of organisational culture, defines it as:

> a pattern of basic assumptions – invented, discovered, or developed by a given group as it learns to cope with its problems of external adaptation and internal integration – that has worked well enough to be considered valid and, therefore, to be taught to new members as the correct way to perceive, think, and feel in relation to those problems. (1985, p. 9)

Much simpler versions are: 'how we do things around here' (Ouchi, 1981) and 'a hidden, yet unifying theme, that provides meaning, direction and mobilisation' (Kilman, 1985 – both quoted in Newman, 1996, p. 14).

Newman (1996), in her comprehensive and eminently readable work on shaping organisational cultures identifies two major themes in the literature:
- the 'corporate culture' approach (Hampden-Turner, 1990) which sees culture as a variable that can be managed in the same way as structures and systems can be: 'It is something which an organisation has, rather than what an organisation is' (Newman, 1996, p. 15).

- the 'interpretive approach' (for example, Sackmann, 1991), where a culture is actively created by organisation members through their social interactions.

One formulation which links closely with Bass and Avolio's Four I approach, where communication, both corporately and individually, is so important, is that when culture:

> represents a web of understanding that we need in order to make sense of and cope with the complexity and confusion of organisational life. This web then gives shape to what we do and the ways in which we do it. (McLean and Marshall, 1988, p. 11)

The transformational leader understands, and is able to cope effectively with, the 'web of understanding' so that he or she has a chance in turning around a problemnatic culture, energising a moribund one, or harnessing the potential of one that is able to deliver the value-based leadership which Nicholls (1999) describes.

Culture is complex

Organisational culture is likely to have the following features:

1. It will manifest itself at various levels and in different ways. Schein's (1985; 2004) model shows three distinct layers, some easily visible and some less so:

> *Artifacts and creations* – visible but often not decipherable:

> - Technology
> - Art
> - Visible and audible behaviour patterns

Values – greater level of awareness:

- Testable in the physical environment
- Testable only by social consensus

Basic assumptions – taken for granted and invisible:

- Relationship to environment
- Nature of reality, time and space
- Nature of human nature
- Nature of human activity
- Nature of human relationships

2. It will be embedded in the informal organisation, demonstrable in the cartoons on the notice board, and the jokes around the coffee maker and so on.

3. It will be taken for granted, and therefore needs to be identified as soon as possible by the leader before they have an opportunity to be sucked into it.

4. Through the culture of a corporate body, or specific team, events are given meaning within a particular worldview.

5. Culture is learned. It is passed on from individual to individual or group to group:

> Culture is like language: we inherit it, learn it, pass it on to others, but in the process we invent new words and expressions - it evolves over time. (Newman, 1996, p. 17)

Usually it evolves, but sometimes it can get stuck for decades. The branch bank at Little Barset-on-the-Hill (if not closed by now in a branch restructuring programme!) will probably have had the same office culture, for good or ill, for many years along the lines of: 'it's the way we do things here'.

It is a building society which Johnson and Scholes utilise in their exploration of strategy formation as a cultural process (Johnson and Scholes, 1989). They believe that a strategy is likely to fail unless the 'recipe' of the culture is understood and taken into account. This 'recipe' is made up of:

- symbols;
- rituals and myths;
- power structures;
- organisational structure;
- control systems; and
- routines.

Each 'ingredient' is likely to be mutually reinforcing, except at times of change, when one or more components will begin to act to change the 'recipe'.

6. It is unrealistic to talk about a single organisational culture in a large entity.

Even with a strong corporate identity, individual sections will be likely to operate in ways which make the overall culture complex and multilayered. This is especially true in professional areas, such as health, social care and education. In the 1990s, for example, the new NHS trusts attempted to create organisational coherence, but always struggled because each area of physical activity within, for example, an acute hospital, is likely to create its own distinct culture.

Russell Mannion and his colleagues have undertaken a comprehensive survey of cultures in acute hospitals in England and describe three main organisational cultures in a multidisciplinary setting, which will be easily recognisable:

- Integrated – when there is a broad-based consensus on the values, beliefs and behaviours within the organisation.
- Differentiated – when different professional groups adhere to their own values and cultures so an integrated approach may be difficult.
- Fragmented – where in extreme cases there may be mutual incomprehension of each other's approaches, or even antagonism (Mannion *et al.,* 2005, p. 30).

In the commercial/industrial world, some companies may consciously strive for variable cultures – for example, a very tight, homogeneous corporate HQ, with work bases (for example, in an IT conglomerate) having quite a different feel from the HQ and each other, precisely because of their different requirements.

Assessing and creating organisational culture at a time of mergers and acquisitions can be particularly convoluted. Merging an acute and community NHS trust with strongly antipathetic management mores is an exercise requiring considerable effort and involvement:

> Achieving cultural change is a complex journey requiring constant revival and review. It also demands unyielding commitment from the trust board. (Spreckley and Hart, 2001, pp. 28-9)

The leader's role

'The only thing of real importance that leaders do', writes Schein (1985), 'is to create and manage culture.' He goes on to say: 'and that unique talent of leaders is to create and manage culture' (p. 2). Culture and leadership, Schein believes, are two sides of the same coin. Leaders, therefore, must:

1. Identify the cultural recipe and how malleable it is.

2. Diagnose its features and its layers (see Handy, 1978; Harrison and Stokes, 1990; Schein, 2004; Goffee and Jones, 2003; Mannion *et al.,* 2005).

3. Ascertain how appropriate the recipe is for the desired strategy.

4. Use transformational values and skills to mould the culture, by acting on ingredients within the recipe. For example, managers going 'back to the floor' and working with staff. Gerry Robinson's BBC TV series demonstrated that

some senior mangers simply do not understand the concept of interacting with the front line, and what a revelation it is to them when they do so.

5. Will not only inspire by example (walk the talk) and learn a great deal, they will also begin a weaving of stories and relationships which create a powerful force for positive development.

Inspirational and influencing leadership will mean using oneself in:

- Living the value and the vision;
- Creating meaning for people;
- Coping creatively with ambiguity and paradox;
- Being aware of the symbolic nature of our actions. As Peters (1989) wrote, 'managing at any time, but more than ever today, is a symbolic activity' (p. 71).
- Changing language and behaviour to model values and goals;
- Conceiving a sense of pathfinding as a team. As one follower said of their leader, who had led them through a series of gruelling challenges, he was a leader:

we followed because he had ideas and because, for a brief moment in our lives, he made us bigger than ourselves. (Hickey, 1992, p. 120)

Barriers to effective leadership

One of the challenges in using current examples of leadership is that no sooner have you written about their glorious achievements than they come crashing down to earth! Corrigan (1999) quotes the example of Martin Taylor, who was brought in by Barclays bank in the late 1990s as the chief executive thought most able to relaunch the bank on a modernisation programme. Taylor was regarded as a major intellect, ideal for the kind of visionary leadership to create the forward drive for a banking institution. Problems with his investment strategy and other issues, however, meant that the board suddenly lost confidence in him. As Corrigan writes: 'understandably, an unexpected and shattering blow to someone used to being adulated for their brain power' (p. 39).

The credit crunch of 2008/09 has demonstrated the difficulty of commercial organisations balancing risk with appropriate safeguards. In the political sphere, Gordon Brown, as Britain's Prime Minister, was greeted with some degree of warmth for his catchphrase: 'not flash, just Gordon', but was then criticised for not being as good a communicator as his predecessor. In the USA, President Obama's inauguration was greeted positively, but as the enormity of the major challenges facing him have continued his ratings have fallen.

A main barrier to effectiveness is the inability to channel the contact with one's own emotions. As Corrigan points out in the example above, leaders can become cut off from the people in their organisation as they move up the career ladder, but they can also cut themselves off from what they are feeling, and the conduits between head and heart, as work crowds out personality. Again using Shakespeare's *Coriolanus* as an example, the armour that he has literally and metaphorically wrapped around himself cannot prevent him from being pierced by the emotions conjured up by his mother and her companions at the gates of Rome:

> Touched just briefly by the humanity that he thought he was separated from, all his separation evaporates and he cannot operate at all. He is destroyed by the contact with the very relationship that he denied could affect him. (Corrigan, 1999, p. 131)

The psychologist, Daniel Goleman believes that the secret behind the success of some people with comparatively few academic gifts and the surprising failures of some with a high IQ 'often lies in the abilities called here emotional intelligence, which include self-control, zeal and persistence, and the ability to motivate oneself' (Goleman, 1996, p. XII – see also the forthcoming *Learning for Practice* manual, *The Intelligent Organisation*). The ability to be in touch with one's thoughts and feelings and connect them; and further to have an empathic relationship with those senior to us, at the same level, our subordinates and customers/stakeholders – without becoming overwhelmed by self-criticism, external criticism or competing demands, is crucial to being an effective leader in a variety of circumstances. This links clearly with the section on self-leadership below.

Clement and Ayers (1976, quoted in Hunt, 1991) defined nine skills that become less or more important as the manager progresses:

Increase in importance by level in the organisation:

- communication;
- decision making;
- planning; and
- ethics.

Decrease or increase and then decrease by level in the organisation:

- human relations;
- counselling;
- supervision;
- technical; and
- management science.

It is not surprising that technical skills become less important (though a continuing empathy with those that produce goods and services does not), but human relations is also seen as a variable, and that is because the leader with a widening span of responsibilities and the need to initiate often painful change processes, must be both completely approachable and human and also utterly distant. This apparent paradox exists because they cannot afford to be 'captured' by any one person or interest group.

Mant's (1984) work on 'Binary' and 'Ternary' managers is helpful here. The former has a two-dimensional approach and is described by Mant as a 'raider'. He or she is obsessed with a 'Route One' approach, to achieve objectives without due process, often in a 'win/lose' situation. The 'Ternary' personality or 'builder' brings in other, higher dimensions to their work. As the external environment gets tougher and change becomes constant, the third dimension of an ethical stance, and a basic fairmindedness, even in tough decisions, is an anchor for the crew tossed about on the waves of change. As the philosopher, Friedrich Nietzsche (1844-1900) wrote: 'he who has a "why" to live by can bear almost any "how"' (quoted in Gilbert and Scragg, 1992, p. 17).

The skills we have considered in the previous section are mainly what Flamholtz and Randall (1989) term 'the outer game of management'. Much more difficult to handle is 'the inner game'. Anyone who watched the enthralling 2001 Wimbledon men's tennis final between Goran Ivanišević and Pat Rafter will know that the former always looked likely to win if he could successfully handle his own internal conflicts between what he wryly called 'the good Goran and the bad Goran'!

Flamholtz and Randall set out three requirements for playing the 'inner game' successfully, namely being able to manage your:

> • own self-esteem so that you derive satisfaction from the things managers are supposed to do – that is, enabling rather than doing;
> • need for direct control over people and results; and
> • need to be liked, so that it does not interfere with performing the managerial role.

Many managers find it very difficult to break away from their trade or professional roots and want to continue in that role, rather than utilising that knowledge and empathy in a wider strategic approach. A valuable perspective on this is Kennedy's report into the child deaths at a Bristol hospital (DoH, 2001) in which John Roylance, former chief executive, is criticised for lacking strategic vision:

> Dr Roylance lacked strategic vision and allowed the directorates to become 'isolated from one another' ... 'The most dangerous management style of all is that of the exercise of power without strategic vision, accompanied by 'divide and rule', it concludes. 'Dr Roylance's style could be so characterised.' (Editorial, Health Service Journal, 2001)

Self-awareness of our strengths and weaknesses and what is required in any one role or situation is vital, and that brings us to the next subject.

Self-leadership

> Know yourself
>
> Socrates (469 BC)
>
> With the realisation of one's own potential and self-confidence in one's ability, one can build a better world
>
> The Dalai Lama (2001, p. 15)

Many practitioners remark that they find it difficult to see themselves assuming a management or leadership role but, in fact, the majority of effective practitioners are good managers through:

- the channelling of appropriate emotions;
- keeping themselves 'in good shape' physically and mentally;
- organising their life – we do not mean being obsessional – and their day, so that they can make decisions and see them through; and
- communicating with those around them – we have all known the brilliant individual who sabotages a project by simply going their own sweet way without bringing people with them.

And effective leaders by:

- developing their own narrative and vision for themselves and their work;
- stretching themselves mentally, emotionally, physically and spiritually;
- pushing forward the boundaries of practice; and
- developing others

The main thrust of eastern and western philosophies can be enshrined in two words, respectively: 'being' and 'becoming'. The ability to harness these two aspects of our lives is a vital ingredient in human development, and therefore in becoming a truly effective leader.

Self-awareness

Gardner (1996), in his depiction of ten modern leaders, quotes Charles Cooley as saying: 'all leadership takes place through the communication of ideas to the minds of others' (p. 41). The leaders Gardner brings into focus weave stories through how they live or what they do; they may extract stories from a group and rework them into a powerful motif; or they may create a new story – especially so for the nation-builder, company-founder and so on.

To weave stories or to transmit ideas, however, we have to have a narrative or concept within us to relate. Ursula LeGuin, in her novel *The Lathe of Heaven* (Le Guin, 1977) tells of a progenitor of stories who is tricked by his therapist so that the latter takes over the dream-making. Because the therapist has no inherent values himself, however, the dreams that become reality are grey and lifeless and begin to suck dry reality itself. As Shakespeare put it: 'The man [or woman] who has no music in himself is fit for treasons, stratagems and spoils' (*The Merchant of Venice*, Act 5 Scene 1).

The music must come from within ourselves, and that can only be developed by an awareness of who we are; what our story is; how we relate to others; and how we can develop a narrative that is of mutual benefit to those we live in community with.

Without in any way advocating a long period of introspection – often almost as destructive as a blithe unawareness of self, it can be useful to consider the broad psychological types; how we perceive reality; and how/why we may feel threatened or secure. People with major insecurities are probably the most difficult to work with, because they neither trust nor like themselves, and therefore, mistrust the motives of others, however well-intentioned.

Rowe (1998) describes two main psychological types in relation to the experience of existence:

> Those of us who experience our self as being a member of a group, as the relationship, the connection between our self and others, see the threat of the annihilation of the self as complete isolation, being left totally, utterly and forever alone thus withering, fading away, disappearing into nothingness.

> Those of us who experience our self as the progressive development of our individuality in terms of clarity, achievement and authenticity see the threat of the annihilation of the self as losing control of your self and your life and falling apart, falling into chaos, fragmenting, crumbling to dust. (p. 25)

This does not mean recommending a long course of psychotherapy! Far from it, an overinvestment in therapy, as opposed to the benefits of a more focused approach, can lead to too much introspection and a separation from colleagues and friends.

What is worth exploring are insights into your personality which assist you to:

- ascertain your areas of strength and developmental needs;
- explore issues around security and insecurity;
- gain insight into how you learn and behave, and how to gain more from experience;
- evaluate your interactions with others and how to become more effective; and
- promote a greater integration between aspects and areas of your life.

Many people are familiar with:

1. The Belbin team matrix (Belbin, 1993) which assesses aptitudes in a team context. This fairly straightforward approach can be a revelation in itself. If you individually, or your team as a whole, produce wonderfully creative ideas but no end products, then you/they may be a 'plant'. Changing the team structure so as to bring in 'shapers' and 'completer finishers' may gain creativity and results together!

2. Myers-Briggs, (see Goldsmith and Wharton, 1993) based on Jung's psychological insights, identifies where each individual is on a continuum of four poles:

Extravert	Introvert
Sensing	Intuitive
Judging	Perceiving
Feeling	Thinking

3. The Enneagram – which is compatible for use with Myers-Briggs uses a nine-point personality profile (see Palmer, 1995; Hampson, 2005). This method gives valuable insights into your personality. It is much more complex than seeing oneself as one 'type',

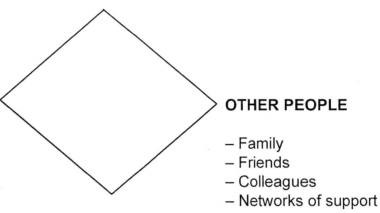

THE OTHER

– God
– Philosophy
– Belief Systems

SELF

– Self awareness
– Being grounded in
core values
– Becoming a more
effective person/leader

OTHER PEOPLE

– Family
– Friends
– Colleagues
– Networks of support

THE CREATED WORLD

– Landscape
– Seascape
– The Animal
– Minerals, plants and so on

Figure 7: The diamond of self and others
(Gilbert 2005, p. 13)

but also, crucially in the work setting, it shows how one is likely to react under pressure; and how one can constructively interact with superiors, subordinates and other stakeholders, with differing personalities.

An holistic approach

> 'If you don't *believe* ... you can't solve these problems and you can't even survive them.' – Harold Macmillan, former British Prime Minister
> (Horne, 1989, p. XIII, emphasis added)

Jagdish Parikh's masterly book, *Managing Your Self: Management by Detached Involvement* (Parikh, 1991) brings together the western 'know yourself' with the eastern 'become yourself' and places the manager in a situation where he or she has a realistic chance of bringing together in a congruent whole:

• self;
• family and community;
• the world of work;

- the internal game; and
- mind, body, emotions, senses and spiritualness.

This approach can lead to becoming a more effective leader and a more complete person. It may also lead to a wholesale change of lifestyle. Some people decide that what they are being asked to do no longer accords with their values. Others, like Mike Grabner, CEO of Energis, decide to leave and start a new working lifestyle at 50 (*The Sunday Times*, 20 May 2001). As Professor Nigel Nicholson of the London Business School states in the same article:

> People are looking at different lifestyles and values. It's an aftermath of the selfishness of the 1980s and 90s and people have come to value a more balanced lifestyle … and are working to live rather than living to work. (p. 32)

Working in Britain in recent years has tended to produce a very one-dimensional workaholic culture. Looking at ourselves holistically we need to consider our:

- *Social/emotional needs*:
    - ✓ relationships: loving and being loved
    - ✓ security
    - ✓ acknowledgement and expression of feelings
    - ✓ kinship
    - ✓ friendships
    - ✓ community involvement
    - ✓ empathy
    - ✓ appreciation of creation

- *Mental or cognitive needs*
    - ✓ opportunities for fresh thinking
    - ✓ reading, and reflection on the texts
    - ✓ planning ahead
    - ✓ creative writing
    - ✓ visualising positive futures
    - ✓ films and plays

- *Spiritual needs*
    - ✓ recommitting to core values
    - ✓ meditation and contemplation
    - ✓ relaxation
    - ✓ exploration of 'being' and 'becoming'

- *Physical needs*
    - ✓ a healthy diet
    - ✓ physical fitness
    - ✓ a sense of well-being and being better able to cope with the pressures of work
    - ✓ gaining asleep and awake time balance

• *Creative needs*
  ✓ using our senses
  ✓ exploring new ways of working/leisure
  ✓ developing creative hobbies

These five elements interact. For example, the leisure firm, Cannons, undertook some partnership work with the mental health charity, Mind. In a survey of the health club's members, 75 per cent used exercise to reduce stress; 67 per cent said they used exercise to maintain their mental health, like lifting 'low' moods; 64 per cent reported improved self-esteem; 64 per cent reported boosted energy levels; 58 per cent reported improved motivation and 35 per cent said their performance at work had also improved. According to Foresight, a Government think-tank, research indicates that mental wellbeing is founded on a number of fairly obvious precepts: connecting – developing relationships with family, friends and colleagues so as to enrich life and bring support; being active and maintaining mobility and fitness; appreciating the beauty of everyday moments and reflecting on them; continuous learning; and altruism – giving to others provides more long-term satisfaction than buying things for ourselves (Foresight, 2008). De Mello (1988) brings together eastern and western philosophy in his work on spirituality. He quotes the great German mystic, Meister Eckhart as saying:

> you should be less concerned about what you have to do and think much more about what you must be. For if your being is good, your work will be of great value. (p. 56)

Learning for the future as well as the present

As Scott (2000) has pointed out, knowledge is 'the only real generic source of differentiation for western companies', and knowledge 'is personalised. It tends to walk out of the building each night'! (p. 6). As organisations transmute, restructure and transmigrate, bonds between firms and workers decay, and the 'savvy knowledge-worker is concerned about their own career, the development of their skills and their personal equity, independent of their immediate employer' (ibid).

Because the organisation (and therefore the corporate and individual role) of today is not that of tomorrow, public companies and private bodies need to appoint people adaptable enough to be competent in the job they have to perform immediately and the role they will have to fulfil in the near future. Managers, to survive and prosper, have to know themselves, their strengths and needs, how they learn, and what will increase their personal and employment proficiency.

In this climate, self-managed learning would appear to be an increasingly potent approach, as opposed to a blanket method, neatly encapsulated by the graffiti which Cunningham quotes in his book on strategic self-managed learning: 'five hundred million lemmings can't be wrong' (1999, p. 3).

Self-managed learning is about individuals managing their own learning – taking responsibility for decisions about:

- what they learn;
- how they learn;
- when they learn;
- where they learn; and, most fundamentally,
- why they learn (Cunningham *et al.*, 2000)

The approach has its own seven 'S' model to match that of the rounded organisation (Bennett, 2000):

- Strategic – long term with the big picture in mind
- Syllabus-free – driven by the real needs of individuals and organisations
- Self-managed – taking responsibility for own learning
- Shared – integrating learning with others and the organisation's needs
- Supported – supporting people in achieving their goals
- Structured – provides a clear structure for learning
- Stretching – demands real, significant, learning.

As a rounded individual, working within an organisation, or working for yourself, you have to manage a number of roles in life and work, and a number of styles, depending on the people and the situation you are interacting with. Ultimately, you also need to be integrated within yourself because it is you that you have to live with most!

Conclusion: Serve to lead

> Trust and credibility come through everyone's observation of the manager's symbolic integrity, not his or her "policy document"

> Tom Peters (1989, p. 149)

'Serve to Lead' is the motto of RMA Sandhurst, Britain's military academy, and in one sense, it may seem an odd adage for such an establishment. In fact, however, leadership is a privilege and a service to be delivered to 'the customer' – whether someone buying a personal computer, or a widow and her children being protected by peacekeeping troops in a war-torn country.

Leadership is not magic. Leaders may be charismatic in the conventional sense, but they don't have to be to be effective in their chosen field. Maureen Oswin, the campaigner for people with disabilities, demonstrated leadership through her knowledge; her determination and persistence to improve the lives of children with disabilities and the light of integrity and dedication which seemed to shine through her.

With the state of society and business (in its widest sense) today, it is in any organisation's best interests to nurture leadership in its myriad forms, so as to move the corporation forward in a positive direction. Because most of us cannot be a Sir John Harvey -Jones, Carly Fiorina, Norman Schwarzkopf, Florence Nightingale and so on, it is worth considering the quietism of leaders – that is:

• Why have so many spiritual leaders – for example, Teresa of Avila, Benedict of Nursia and Thomas Merton – had such a seminal effect on their contemporaries and down the ages, when they lived a secluded life?

• How many of your colleagues are well-respected leaders in their local communities/leisure time activities and so on, and yet work clearly does not 'turn them on'? How can we wake 'the sleeping giant' of each individual's potential?

If we accept that people need to be good leaders and good followers in different situations, it is sensible to look at the views of their followers – the consumers of leadership – and how they define leadership. James Kouzes and Barry Posner (1990, 2007), in their research on leadership credibility, state that: 'leadership is in the eye of the follower' (p. 29).

The attributes they identified were:

• *Integrity*

People want to work with someone they believe is honest and truthful, and has character and convictions. We do not want to serve someone who is only fuelling their own career. When the chips are down, and the shots ring out, do you and your colleagues cover your own backs or protect those of your comrades?! Kouzes and Posner write that:

> if a leader behaves in ways consistent with his or her stated values and beliefs, then we believe we can entrust to that person our careers, our security, even our lives. (p. 30)

Trust works both ways, and one of the most important characteristics is the trust leaders display in those who work for them.

• *Competence*

This does not necessarily mean technical competence, and indeed, clinging onto professional or technical skills at all costs may become a barrier to effective leadership. But, people look towards leaders who have an empathy with the 'customer'; the product or service being created, and those who deliver it; have a track record of success; and are able to inject extra ingredients – for example, strategic or marketing skills – into a firm which has a good product, but is poor at selling it.

• *The ability to create a vision*

Leaders must know where they are going and to what horizon they are pathfinding people to. Of course, this vision creation can be a false dawn. Marconi's switch into majoring on telecommunications led to their marked decline during 2001. But to do nothing in a world of change can be disastrous with the added problem of complacency, and lack of awareness when danger surfaces. The modern manager needs to have the capacity for 'helicopter vision' to get above the ground level and scan the wider perspectives. But they must also be aware of the need to 'land' and communicate their vision to those still 'on the ground'.

• *Inspiration*

Both to keep going when things get tough, and/or remain a daily grind, or to cope with the seismic shift required at times of change, the leader must create a climate of inspiration (as well as perspiration) and generate excitement and passion. If the leader appears to have little enthusiasm for the task in hand, or to strike out for the new world ahead, why should anyone else?

We would like add two further attributes:

• *Emotional connection and embodied leadership*

Allied to inspiration is emotional connection and integration. Work and life are two sides of the same coin and the emotional content of each invades the other. Following the attacks on New York (9/11), Rudi Guiliani, then the Mayor of New York, not only went into his city (placing himself physically at risk while expressing in a very personal way his solidarity with the victims, the bereaved and the rescue parties), but also spoke the right words – epitomising the spirit of the city and its people. Leaders have to go out in front but they have to bring others with them – or they are very lonely and not much use to anybody! Leaders need to be translators, communicators, bridge builders and embodied (Webster, 2001; Guiliani ; 2003).

• *The ability to build effective teams*

Although Hollywood movies still persist with the myth of the singleton hero, riding into town, more realistic is the film, modelled on the Japanese 'Seven Samurai' – that is, 'The Magnificent Seven'. Leaders usually achieve lasting success through the teams they build in the present, and teams they leave behind them when they move out of town.

John Alban-Metcalfe and Beverly Alimo-Metcalfe, in their latest research, speak about an essential connection between the personal qualities and values which a leader has; the leadership competencies they develop; and the 'engaging' behaviours which they demonstrate. Nelson Mandela (see Biography 1) provided iconic leadership during his days of captivity. He did not need to 'do' anything, his 'being' was enough to inspire people nationally and internationally. This could be said of many spiritual leaders. But running a complex organisation in the modern world will require a set of competencies, which embrace the transactional and transformational. Finally, leaders cannot do everything themselves. They depend on teams of people, and the customer experience is found at the front line as the Alimo-Metcalfe's say, 'competencies can be likened to Brighton Pier, very fine in their own way, but not a good way of getting to France!' (Alban-Metcalfe and Alimo-Metcalfe, 2009a, p. 17).

Kouzes and Posner (1990) add five fundamental actions which people said built the credibility of those they wanted to lead them:

- Know your constituents.
- Stand up for your beliefs.
- Speak with passion.
- Lead by example.
- Conquer yourself.

They quote the Himalayan climber, Jim Whitaker: 'you never conquer a mountain. Mountains can't be conquered, you conquer yourself, your hopes, your fears' (p. 33).

In the end, in a rapidly changing world where you are almost certain to lose some battles along the way – internal and/or external – whatever your façade of confidence may show, it comes down to us:

- What we believe;
- How we demonstrate it;
- The vision we have and how we articulate it;
- Our ability to take people with us; and
- How we learn and how we encourage learning.

Bobby Kennedy once pondered that the Gross National Product of a nation contained nothing of fundamental value in terms of building a better future for its citizens. In a very different context, Pierre d'Harcourt explored essential values in relating his experiences in Buchenwald concentration camp. In the end, he believed: 'only one thing prevailed, strength of character. Cleverness, creativeness, learning, all went down; only real goodness survived' (cited in Philpot, 1986, p. 153).

Individuals, organisations and nations must ask: What are we about and why, and how do we do what we set out to achieve? Many of the companies lauded by Peters and Waterman have now fallen from grace – empires rise and fall. Socrates' challenge to us all still resonates:

> Citizens of Athens, aren't you ashamed to care so much about making all the money you can, and advancing your reputation and prestige, while for truth and wisdom and the improvement of your souls you have no thought or care.
>
> 'Crito', cited in Hollis (2001, p. 92)

Training and Development

Introduction

In Part Two of the manual we present a range of exercises. Here you will find details of activities that can be used as the basis of training courses or staff development exercises.

Various exercises refer to presentation slides, these are to be found in the appendix at the end of the manual.

The exercises are described in such a way as to be useful to both experienced trainers and those with little or no experience of running training sessions. It is likely that more experienced trainers will want to adapt materials to suit their own purposes and their own styles of working. However, less experienced trainers are more likely to want to follow each of the exercises step by step. The materials are presented in this way so that they can be used with maximum flexibility according to need.

STEP Factors

Aim

This is an exercise which asks participants to identify and evaluate the:

- Sociological
- Technological
- Economic
- Political

factors which affect their business as a whole and their particular firm/care home/retail outlet/school and so on, within the overall sector in which they operate.

Materials

Flip chart paper and pens; Blutack or masking tape; Slide 1

Timing

This exercise is likely to take about 70 minutes.

Introduction:	5 minutes
Group work:	25 minutes
Feedback and discussion:	35 minutes
Summary and conclusion:	5 minutes

Activity

- Explain to the group that no individual, team or organisation is an 'island', and that their particular activity takes place within a complex milieu of social, technological, economic and political factors which are constantly changing and interacting (see Slide 1). Emphasise that leadership involves being able to see one's organisation in terms of the 'big picture', and that then is likely to include the wider sociological, technological, economic and political factors.

- Next, divide the group into subgroups of 4 to 6 people, provide them with marker pens and flip chart paper, and ask them to identify, write down and discuss the STEP factors which affect their organisation. Alternatively, you might want to divide the main group into four subgroups and ask each group to look at one particular set of factors, and then bring those together in the plenary session.

• When the groups have formulated their ideas, bring them together for a plenary discussion session, and ask them to present and discuss their findings in turn. This should form the basis of a wide-ranging discussion of some of the key issues relating to the external environment and its influence on management and leadership.

• Use the last few minutes to sum up the main points of learning or ask the group to do so.

SWOT Analysis

Aim

This SWOT analysis exercise assists the group to identify the:

- Strengths
- Weaknesses
- Opportunities
- Threats

which face the team and/or the organisation as a whole. It presents SWOT analysis as a useful planning and decision-making tool which can be very helpful in the development of leadership skills.

NB Depending on the circumstances, you may wish to handle this exercise as the SWOT analysis of a particular team or teams, or for the organisation as a whole.

Materials

Flip chart paper and pens; Blutack or masking tape; Slide 2.

Timing

This exercise is likely to take about 70 minutes.

Introduction:	5 minutes
Group work:	25 minutes
Feedback and discussion:	35 minutes
Summary and conclusion:	5 minutes

Activity

- Begin by explaining that this exercise will give participants the opportunity to use a well-established analytical tool to look at their team, project, organisation or whatever. Make it clear to the group that having an overview of strengths, weaknesses, opportunities and threats is an important basis for well-informed leadership.

- Divide the main group into subgroups of 4 to 6 people and ask them to undertake a SWOT analysis of the team, organisation, project or whatever you decide is the appropriate object of your attentions. Alternatively, you may wish to divide the main group into 4 subgroups and allocate one aspect (strengths, weaknesses, opportunities or threats) to each of the groups. This alternative version can be useful if you are short of time, as it tends to take less time than the full version where each group carries out a whole SWOT analysis.

• If participants are not familiar with the idea of SWOT analysis, use Slide 2 to explain its basis.

• It is important that members step 'outside the box', so that they look at their team and/or organisation from what it feels like to be both inside the entity and outside it – experiencing the organisation as a customer, partner agency, user of the service, supplier and so on.

• After approximately 25 minutes, bring the group back together for a plenary discussion, and again encourage people to look at the organisation from as many different perspectives as possible. An alternative would be for people to tell stories about the organisation that they have picked up – for example, a customer they encountered in the car park, and so on.

• In taking feedback from this exercise, it is important not to get bogged down in the detail of what points or issues were raised in the actual SWOT analysis. Emphasis should be placed on what the actual exercise tells us – that is, what patterns emerge, what conclusions can be drawn, what lessons can be learned and so on.

• Use the last few minutes to sum up the main learning points or ask the group to do so.

Images of Leadership

Aim

This exercise is designed to ascertain what fundamental images the word and concept of leadership evoke amongst the individuals in the group. It should help participants to develop a clearer idea of what leadership means to them.

Materials

Flip chart paper and pens available if people wish to draw their image; Blutack or masking tape; Slide 3.

Timing

This exercise is likely to take 60 to 70 minutes.

Introduction:	5 minutes
Individual work:	10 to 15 minutes
Feedback and discussion:	30 minutes
Summary and conclusion:	5 minutes

Activity

• Explain to the group that any concept, such as leadership, is likely to evoke immediate images in people's minds as well, perhaps, as experiences from their past. Depending on people's experience, and/or their cultural background, they may well have deep-seated issues which they may need to consider. You may find it useful to display Slide 3 at this point.

• Next, ask the group to spend 10 to 15 minutes 'getting in touch' with their images of what the word or concept of leadership conjures up for them. Ask them to relax, breathe deeply, think of the word or concept, 'leadership' in their minds and allow whatever occurs to them to come into their mind and then record that on paper. Each individual should be asked to write down on paper, or perhaps draw, whatever words or images are immediately real to them. It is important to note that it is really useful for this exercise to be as much as possible from the heart and the gut, rather than the head.

• Next, ask the individual participants to go into pairs (or trios) and to compare notes, identifying any key issues or significant points to have emerged from the images they have conjured up. This should take a further 10 to 15 minutes.

• Next, ask for volunteers from the group as a whole or from each pair/trio, depending on the size of the group, to feed back and share their images of leadership. This should then form the basis of a plenary discussion to draw out the main learning points.

• Use the last few minutes to sum up the key issues or ask the group to do so.

Leadership Recognition

Aim

This exercise helps you identify leadership characteristics in:

1. People you work with currently.
2. People you have worked with.
3. Individuals currently engaged in public life through politics, sport, business, welfare and so on.
4. Leadership figures from history.

Materials

Flip chart paper and pens; Blutack or masking tape.

Timing

This exercise is likely to take about 80 minutes.

Introduction:	5 minutes
Groupwork:	25 minutes
Feedback and discussion:	35 minutes
Summary and conclusion:	5 minutes

Activity

• Begin by explaining to the group that this exercise is geared towards helping participants identify the characteristics of leadership and that this is to be done by considering well-known leaders from public life.

• Next, divide the group into pairs and ask each individual to identify two people (one woman and one man), from the present or the past, whom they would identify as a leader. After a few minutes, each individual should then be asked to share his or her choices within the pair. They should also discuss the reasons for their choices and, if people find that they have chosen historical figures, it might be worth their while exploring whether the sharp light of today makes it more difficult to think of a current figure as a leader.

• After about 10 minutes, ask the participants to think of four qualities or skills which make the people they identified stand out as a leader and to discuss these briefly with their partners within the pairs. This should also take about 10 minutes.

• Next, reconvene the main group for a plenary discussion in which the pairs should share their choices of leader and the qualities and skills with the full group. Use this session as the basis of a discussion which identifies the main characteristics of a leader and any debates or disputes about what makes for a good leader.

• Use the last few minutes to sum up the main learning points or ask the group to do so.

Leadership Biographies

Aim

This exercise can be used as an alternative to Exercise 4 or, if you have plenty of time to devote to this subject, as a follow-up to it. It involves identifying leadership characteristics by looking at biographical summaries of well-established leaders.

Materials

Flip chart paper and pens; Blutack or masking tape; Copies of one or more biographies (which are located in the appendix at the end of this manual).

Timing

This exercise is likely to take about 80 minutes (longer if more than one biography is chosen).

Introduction:	5 minutes
Individual work:	10 minutes
Groupwork:	25 minutes
Feedback and discussion:	35 minutes
Summary and conclusion:	5 minutes

Activity

• Begin by explaining that this exercise involves looking at one or more well-established leaders to see what we can learn about leadership from considering key points about their life and their approach to being a leader. Make the point that biographies from outside people's immediate experience can be very illuminating and can aid lateral thinking. Next, issue a copy of one of the biography summaries to each participant. You may issue a copy of the same biography to everyone or you may wish to use more than one of the 12. Please note, however, that the more you choose, the richer the discussion is likely to be – but also, the longer it is likely to be. If you choose the plural option, you may therefore have to rely on good chairing skills to make sure that the exercise does not overrun its time allocation.

• Allow about 10 minutes for each participant to read the biographical summary and to make notes about what they regard as the key aspects or significant points.

• Next, divide the main group into subgroups and ask them to identify, and note down, the main features of successful leadership, as suggested by their reading of the biographical summaries.

• After 20 to 25 minutes, reconvene that main group for a plenary feedback and discussion session. This should allow a number of important points about what makes for a good leader to emerge. In this way participants can be helped to recognise what they may have in common with one or more established leaders and what skills or attitudes they will need to nurture and develop over time.

• Use the last few minutes to sum up the main learning points or ask the group to do so.

Styles of Leadership

Aim

The aim of the exercise is to identify styles of leadership and to consider what style is appropriate in what circumstances.

Materials

Flip chart paper and pens; Blutack or masking tape; Slide 4

Timing

This exercise is likely to take about 70 minutes.

Introduction:	5 minutes
Groupwork:	25 minutes
Feedback and discussion:	35 minutes
Summary and conclusion:	5 minutes

Activity

• Begin by drawing attention to the content in Part One of the manual on situational leadership, and the fact that managers need to consider three interrelated factors:

1. Their own character and qualities.
2. Those of their subordinates.
3. The situation they find themselves in at the time.

• You should begin by displaying Slide 4 to indicate the four styles, or ask the group to identify the styles of leadership that they perceive. They may well come up with some additional styles beyond those mentioned in the manual, and/or different names for the four styles outlined.

• Next, divide the main group into subgroups of 4 to 6 people and ask them to consider which leadership style they would regard as suitable in working i) with different people and ii) in different circumstances. They should note down on what basis they would make such decisions. Alternatively, it may be useful to encourage group members to use specific, real-life examples, though it is important, if this is done, that issues of confidentiality are very clearly set out.

• After about 25 minutes, reconvene the main group for a plenary feedback and discussion session. This should provide the opportunity to help participants to appreciate the importance of recognising styles of leadership and being clear about which style(s) they aspire to and why.

• Use the last few minutes to summarise the key learning points or ask the group to do so.

Motivation

Aim

This leads on from Exercise 6 and asks group members to examine what factors they feel motivate employees.

Materials

Flip chart paper and pens, Blutack or masking tape; Slide 5

Timing

This exercise is likely to take about 80 minutes.

Introduction:	5 minutes
Work in pairs:	10 minutes
Groupwork:	25 minutes
Feedback and discussion:	35 minutes
Summary and conclusion:	5 minutes

Activity

• Begin by displaying Slide 5 on theories X, Y and Z on employee motivation and briefly explain its contents. Next divide the group into pairs and ask them to examine the applicability of these theories to the people they manage currently. Allow about 10 minutes for this.

• Next, ask the pairs to join together into groups of four or six. Ask them to identify as many strategies for motivating people as they can, strategies to help staff raise their performance and retain their services and skills. Suggest to the group that they may find it helpful to start with their own motivation – that is, by considering what makes them tick in general and what inspires them to 'go the extra mile' when they need to.

• After about 25 minutes, reconvene the main group for a plenary feedback and discussion session. This should present opportunities for participants to develop a good understanding of theories of motivation and to be clear about practical strategies that can be used to get the best out of people through motivation.

• Use the last few minutes to sum up the main learning points or ask the group to do so.

Leadership and Management

Aim

This exercise examines both the differences between management and leadership and the synergies between them. The assumption is that modern organisations need both sound management and effective leadership if they are to maximise their potential.

Materials

Flip chart paper and pens, Blutack or masking tape: Slides 6 and 7 (7 is optional).

Timing

This exercise is likely to take about 80 minutes.

Introduction:	5 minutes
Groupwork 1:	10 to 15 minutes
Feedback and discussion 1:	20 minutes
Groupwork 2:	10 to 15 minutes
Feedback and discussion 2:	20 minutes
Summary and conclusion:	5 minutes

Activity

• Display Slide 6, which shows the origin of the terms leadership and management.

• Divide the main group into subgroups of 4 to 6 people. Issue each group with a sheet of flip chart paper and a marker pen. Ask them to draw a line down the middle of the page and ask them to consider:

    1. What managers do.
    2. What leaders do.

• They should record their comments relating to 1 on the left-hand side of the paper and those relating to 2. on the right-hand side. Inform the group that they should ask for a a second sheet of paper if they complete their first, rather than write on the other side. This is because the sheets are going to be displayed on the wall later in the exercise.

• After only 10 to 15 minutes, ask the groups to display their sheets on the walls around the room, using blutack or masking tape (if you have permission to do this, lay them out on tables otherwise and then ask the participants to wander around the room looking at what their colleagues have come up with).

• After a few minutes of this, reconvene the main group for a plenary feedback and discussion session to explore the findings of each of the small groups. You may also find it helpful to display Slide 7 during this session. This should take about 20 minutes.

• Next, ask the participants to return to their groups and to consider whether, individually, they feel more comfortable in a management or a leadership function, and how each individual can do two things differently to increase their abilities as a leader, if they see themselves as a manager, or as a manager, if they see themselves as a leader.

• After 10 to 15 minutes, once again reconvene the main group for a plenary feedback and discussion session in order to identify common themes, significant differences, lessons to be learned and so on.

• Use the last few minutes to sum up the main points of learning or ask the group to do so.

Balancing Task: Team and Individual

Aim

This exercise is designed to help people consider the balance between the task, the coherence of the team and the needs of individuals, and how these interact with one another.

Materials

Flip chart paper and pens; blutack or masking tape; copies of the Worksheet – Balancing Task: Team and Individual; Slides 8-11.

Timing

This exercise is likely to take about 70 minutes.

Introduction:	5 minutes
Groupwork:	25 minutes
Feedback and discussion:	35 minutes
Summary and conclusion:	5 minutes

Activity

• First, explain to the group, using Slides 8-11, that this simple, but effective concept helps leaders to ensure that:

   1. The task(s) to be accomplished is always kept firmly in the forefront of people's minds, and is successfully accomplished.
   2. The whole team is on board and working together.
   3. Because a team is only as strong as its weakest link, the needs of individuals are attended to and people are helped to develop.

• Second, divide the group (as far as possible) into functional subgroups – actual teams or people doing similar work – and ask them to identify one or more tasks they are facing at work at the moment. Next, the group should choose one of the tasks identified and concentrate on it. Ask the group to identify the steps they need to undertake to achieve their identified task, and then how this will affect the team and individuals. The worksheet can be used for this purpose.

• Explain to them that their group task is to envisage how they would ensure that they keep all three areas (task, team and individual) in alignment, with the fulfilment of the task in prime position, during the stresses and strains of fulfilling that task.

• If they complete this in relation to one task during the time allowed, ask them to begin the process again with another task from the ones initially identified.

• After about 25 minutes, reconvene the main group for a plenary feedback and discussion session. This should provide opportunities for linking theory to practice by exploring how the model can be used to address real-life situations.

• Use the last few minutes to sum up the main learning points, or ask the group to do so.

Balancing Task: Team and Individual

1. Briefly describe the task to be achieved:

2. What steps would you need to take to achieve this task?

3. What impact would your actions have on i) the team and ii) the individuals concerned?

Obstacles to Leadership

Aim

This exercise asks individuals and the group to identify obstacles to leadership and how these can be overcome.

Materials

Flip chart paper and pens, Blutack or masking tape; Slide 12.

Timing

This exercise is likely to take about 80 minutes.

Introduction:	5 minutes
Work in pairs:	10 minutes
Groupwork:	25 minutes
Feedback and discussion:	35 minutes
Summary and conclusion:	5 minutes

Activity

• First, begin by asking each individual member to think over their career and identify the obstacles to development that they encountered at each step, either within themselves or externally.

• Second, divide the group into pairs to discuss those obstacles with one another. Allow about 10 minutes for this.

• Third, ask the pairs to team up to make groups of 4 or 6. Once in their groups, they should share amongst themselves the range of obstacles they have identified. They should then remain in their groups to identify how they would overcome such obstacles within their own resources, and what resources they would need externally.

• Fourth, after about 25 minutes, reconvene the main group for a plenary feedback and discussion session to gather all the issues together. There will be both internal and external obstacles which people identify, but ask them to concentrate most especially on the open 'inner game of management' as defined by Flamholtz and Randall (Slide 12 can be used for this purpose).

• Fifth, use the last few minutes to sum up the main learning points or ask the group to do so.

Identifying One's Own Needs in Self-leadership

Aim

This exercise asks each individual to identify his or her own developmental needs and to come up with a brief personal action plan.

Materials

Flip chart, paper and marker pen or other writing board; Copies of the Worksheet – Identifying One's Own Needs in Self-leadership; Slides 13-14

Timing

This exercise is likely to take about 80 minutes.

Introduction and presentation of slides:	10 minutes
Individual work:	20 minutes
Work in pairs:	20 minutes
Feedback and discussion:	25 minutes
Summary and conclusion:	5 minutes

Activity

• Begin by using slides 13-14 to help participants focus on their immediate and longer-term developmental needs. The first slide shows the interaction between the self and others; and the third considers five areas of needs and development.

• Next divide the group into pairs for about 20 minutes, and ask them to help each other identify:

1. Where they see themselves at the moment.
2. How they see themselves developing.
3. What obstacles they face.
4. What they need to do to develop in the five areas of need:

   i) social/emotional;
   ii) mental or cognitive;
   iii) spiritual;
   iv) physical; and
   v) creative.

• Point out that i) the normal rules of confidentiality apply; and ii) no-one is obliged to reveal any information they do not wish to share.

• Using the Worksheet as a framework, ask the participants to identify one issue from each of these five areas and put down what they are going to do to develop positively in this area, how they are going to do it and when, and how they will know when they have attained a positive improvement.

• Please note that you will need to be aware that this could easily evoke a number of emotional issues from the present or the past, and you will need to be able to deal constructively with this.

• Next, combine the pairs into groups of 4 or 6, to expand their range of issues. The aim here should not simply be to repeat discussions already held in the pairs, but rather to identify patterns, emerging themes, conclusions that can be drawn and so on.

• After about 20 minutes, reconvene the main group for a plenary feedback and discussion session. This should allow participants to get an overview of self-leadership and what is involved in taking responsibility for one's own development.

• Use the last few minutes to sum up the main learning points or ask the group to do so.

Identifying One's Own Needs in Self-leadership

i) social/emotional

ii) mental or cognitive

iii) spiritual

iv) physical

v) creative

Part Three

Conclusion

This manual has presented a wide range of resource materials, from the background materials in Part One through to the detailed training exercises laid out in Part Two. The role of Part Three of the manual is relatively straightforward – simply to draw together the main strands of the pack and to point you in the right direction for future learning.

This part of the manual will therefore:

- summarise the main themes that have emerged;

- present ideas for further development through recommended reading, access to relevant organisations, websites and so on;

- provide details of all the books and articles referred to in the text.

Leadership

Perhaps the most important point to note in relation to leadership is that it is an essential part of organisational success. Leadership involves helping the organisation make sure it is focused on its goals and is doing all it reasonably can to motivate its employees to achieve those goals. Without such a focus it is highly unlikely that an organisation will achieve significant success.

Leadership helps to give a sense of direction to an organisation and to its staff and managers. It does this by clarifying a 'vision' – an understanding of what they want the organisation to be like, as such a vision is an important part of motivating and inspiring employees to work towards making the vision a reality.

Leadership is closely linked to management but it is more than management. That is, it goes beyond simply making sure that the necessary systems are in place and are working effectively. Leadership is a driving force that helps bring out the best in any organisation's most important resource – its people. The term, 'transformational' is often used to distinguish between leadership and management. That is, leadership can play an important part in transforming the organisation concerned, helping it to adapt to changing circumstances and constantly improving, as far as possible.

Perhaps more than anything else, leadership is about shaping organisational culture. This involves influencing the culture to make it a supportive and dynamic one in which staff feel valued and supported and are thus strongly motivated to play a significant part in achieving the organisation's goals, now, and in the future.

Recommended Reading

The following texts give a general overview of management theory:

Clegg, S., Kornberger, M. and Pitsis, T. (2005) *Managing and Organisations: An Introduction to Theory and Practice*, London: SAGE.

Clutterbuck, D. and Crainer, S. (1990) *Makers of Management*, London: Macmillan – now Palgrave Macmillan.

Graham, P. (1991) *Integrative Management: Creating Unity from Diversity*, Oxford: Blackwell.

Handy, C. (1985) *Understanding Organisations*, Harmondsworth: Penguin.

Lawrence, P. and Elliott, K. (1985) *Introducing Management*, Harmondsworth: Penguin.

Lorenz, C. and Leslie, N. (eds) (1992) *The Financial Times on Management*, London: Pitman.

Scragg, T. (2009) *Managing At The Front Line: A Handbook For Managers In Social Care Agencies*, 2nd edn, Brighton: Pavilion.

Stewart, R. (1985) *The Reality of Management*, Revised edn, London: Heinemann.

The following texts relate to leadership as a specific issue:

Adair, J. (1988) *Effective Leadership*, London: Pan.

Blanchard, K., Zigarmi, P. and Zigarmi, D. (1986) *Leadership and the One Minute Manager*, London: William Collins.

Gilbert, P. (2005) *Leadership: Being Effective and Remaining Human*, Lyme Regis: Russell House Publishing.

Gill, R. (2006) *Theory and Practice of Leadership,* London, SAGE.

Goffee, R. and Jones, G. (2006) *Why Should Anyone Be Led By You?: What it Takes to be an Authentic Leader*, Boston, MA: Harvard Business School Press.

Grint, P. (2005) *Leadership: Limits and Possibilities*, Basingstoke: Palgrave Macmillan.

Holbeche, L. (2005) *The High Performance Organisation: Creating Dynamic Stability and Sustainable Success,* Oxford: Elseiver Butterworth-Heinemann.

Hunt, J. (1991) *Leadership: A New Synthesis,* London: SAGE.

Kotter, J.P. (1996) *Leading Change*, Boston, MA: Harvard Business School Press.

Kouzes, J.M. and Posner. B.Z.(2007) *The Leadership Challenge*, 4th edn, San Francisco, CA: Jossey-Bass

Maxwell, J.C. (2006) *The 360° Leader,* Nashville, TN: Thomas Nolan.

Smith, P. and Peterson, M. (1988) *Leadership, Organisations and Culture*, London: SAGE.

Organisational culture and quality management are dealt with in these books:

Dale, B. and Plunkett, J. (eds) (1990), *Managing Quality*, London: Philip Allan.

Hampden-Turner, C. (1990) *Corporate Culture*, London: Hutchinson.

Monroe-Faure, L. and Monroe-Faure, M. (1992) *Implementing Total Quality Management*, London: Pitman.

Newman, J. (1996) *Shaping Organisational Cultures in Local Government*, London: Pitman.

Schein, E. (2004) *Organisational Culture and Leadership*, San Francisco, CA: Jossey-Bass.

Storey, J. (ed.) (2004) *Leadership Organisations: Current Issues and Key Trends*, London: Routledge.

The interaction between management and leadership is explored in:

Kotter, J.P. (1988) *The Leadership Factor,* New York, NY: The Free Press.

Kotter, J.P. (1990) *A Force for Change: How Leadership Differs from Management*, New York, NY: The Free Press.

Peters, T. and Austin, N. (1985) *A Passion for Excellence: The Leadership Difference*, London: William Collins.

Strategic management is featured in:

Adair, J. (2003) *Effective Strategic Leadership*, London: Pan Books,

Hussey, D. (1998) *The Strategic Decision Challenge*, Chichester: John Wiley.

Johnson, G. and Scholes, K. (1989) *Exploring Corporate Strategy: Text and Cases*, London: Prentice-Hall.

Some interesting ways of looking at leadership are:

Birch, P. and Clegg, B. (1996) *Imagination Engineering: The Toolkit for Business Creativity*, London: Pitman.

Corrigan, P. (1999) *Shakespeare on Management*, London: Kogan Page.

Gardner, H. (1996) *Leading Minds: An Anatomy of Leadership*, London: HarperCollins.

Keegan, J. (ed.) (1987) *The Mask of Command*, London: Jonathan Cape.

Wheatley, M. (1999) *Leadership and the New Science*, San Francisco, CA: Berrett-Koehler.

For self-managed learning:

Cunningham, I., Bennett, B. and Dawes, G. (eds) (2000), *Self-managed Learning in Action*, Aldershot: Gower.

An overview of project management is contained in:

Turner, R. (1993) *The Handbook of Project-based Management*, Maidenhead: McGraw-Hill.

Other useful texts include:

Casey, C. (2002) *Critical Analysis of Organizations: Theory, Practice, Revitilization*, London: SAGE.

Hayward, S. (2005) *Women Leading*, Basingstoke: Palgrave Macmillan.

Thompson, N. (2009) *People Skills*, 3rd edn, Basingstoke: Palgrave Macmillan.

Thompson, N. and Bates, J. (eds) (2009) *Promoting Workplace Well-being*, Basingstoke: Palgrave Macmillan.

Journals include:

The International Journal of Leadership in Public Services, Pier Professional Publishing

International Journal of Leadership Studies, Regent University School of Global Leadership & Entrepreneurship

Journal of Leadership and Organizational Studies, SAGE Publications

Journal of Leadership Studies, Wiley Interscience

Leadership & Organization Development Journal, Emerald

Organisations and Websites

Organisations

Chartered Institute of Personnel and Development
CIPD House
151, The Broadway
Wimbledon
London, SW19 1JQ
Tel 020 8612 6200
Fax 020 8612 620
www.cipd.co.uk

Chartered Management Institute
Management House
Cottingham Road
Corby
NN17 1TT
Tel 01536 204222
Fax 01536 201651
www.managers.org.uk

Institute of Leadership and Management
Stowe House
Netherstowe
Lichfield
WS13 6TJ
Tel: 01543 251346
www.i-l-m.com

The Open Cloister
Worth Abbey
Paddockhurst Road
Turner's Hill
RH10 4SB
Tel 01342 710318
Fax: 01342 710311
Email toc@worthabbey.net

The Work Foundation
21 Palmer Street
London
SW1H 0AD

Websites

The Chartered Institute of Personnel and Development
www.cipd.co.uk

The website of the foremost professional organisation relating to human resource development. A very useful starting point for information about a wide range of issues relating to human resources.

Human Solutions
www.humansolutions.org.uk

Information about 'people problems' in the workplace, offering useful insights to leaders and managers.

National Nursing Leadership Project
www.nursingleadership.co.uk

An invaluable site for anyone interested in leadership in nursing and health care.

The Open Cloister
www.worthabbey.net/cloister

Website of a centre which runs a number of courses which look at spirituality in the workplace

Well-being Zone
www.well-beingzone.com

An online community for everyone interested in and committed to well-being in its various forms, including workplace well-being.

NB These sites are correct at the time of publication, but may be liable to change over time.

References

Adair, J. (1983) *Effective Leadership*, Aldershot: Gower.

Adair, J. (2002) *Inspiring Leadership*, London: Thorogood.

Adair, J. (2003) *Effective Strategic Leadership*, London: Pan Books.

Adair, J. (2005) *How to Grow Leaders*, London: Kogan Page.

Adams, S. (1997) *The Dilbert Principle*, London: Macmillan – now Palgrave Macmillan.

Alban-Metcalfe, J. and Alimo-Metcalfe, B. (2009a) Engaging Leadership Part 1: Competencies are Like Brighton Pier, *The International Journal of Leadership in Public Services*, 5 (1).

Alban-Metcalfe, J. and Alimo-Metcalfe, B. (2009b) Engaging Leadership Part 2: An Integrated Model of Leadership Development', *The International Journal of Leadership in Public Services*, 5 (2).

Allen, R., Gilbert, P. and Onyett, S. (2009) *Leadership for Personalisation and Social Inclusion in Mental Health,* London: SCIE.

Argyris, C. (1953) 'Integrating the Individual and the Organisation', *The Personnel Journal*, 32(2).

Argyris, C. and Schön, D. (1974) *Theory in Practice*, San Francisco, CA: Jossey-Bass

Aris, S. and Gilbert, P. (2007) 'Organisational Health: Engaging the Heart of the Organisation', in Coyte, M.E., Gilbert, P. and Nicholls, V. (ed.) (2007).

Atkinson, D. (2001) 'Touching the Lives of Thousands of Children, Obituary on Maureen Oswin', *Community Care*, 9–15 August

Bass, B. and Avolio, B. (1994) *Improving Organisational Effectiveness Through Transformational Leadership*, London, SAGE.

Bates, B. and Gilbert, P. (2008) I Wanna Tell You a Story: Leaders as Storytellers, *The International Journal of Leadership in Public Services*, 4 (2).

Belbin, R.M. (1993) *Team Roles at Work*, London: Butterworth Heinemann.

Benedict of Nursia (circa 540 AD), 'The Rule of St Benedict' in Fry, T. (ed.) (1982).

Bennett, B. (2000) 'Self managed learning in organisations', in Cunningham, I., Bennett, B. and Dawes, G. (eds),.(2000)

Bennis, W. (1989) *On Becoming a Leader*, New York, NY: Addison-Wesley.

Blake, R. (1997) *The Conservative Party from Peel to Churchill*, London: Arrow Books

Blanchard, K. and Johnson, S. (1983) *The One Minute Manager,* London: HarperCollins.

Blanchard, K., Zigarmi, P., and Zigarmi, D. (1986) *Leadership and the One Minute Manager,* London: Collins.

Boyatzis, R. and McKee, A. (2005) *Resonant Leadership*, Boston, MA: Harvard Business School Press.

British Association of Social Workers (BASW) (2002) *A Revised Code of Ethics for Social Work,* Birmingham: BASW

Burns, J.M. (1978) *Leadership,* New York, NY: Harper & Row.

Butler, C. (ed.) (1999) *Basil Hume: By His Friends*, London: HarperCollins.

Cabinet Office, (2001) *Choosing the Right Fabric: A Framework for Performance Information*, London: HMSO.

Cable, V. (2009) *The Storm: The World Economic Crisis and What it Means*, London: Atlantic Books.

Carlson, S. (1951) *Executive Behaviour: A Study of the Workload and the Working Methods of Managing Directors*, Stockholm, Sweden: Strombergs.

Catholic

74

Catholic Bishops' Conference of England and Wales (1996) *The Common Good and the Catholic Church's Social Teaching*, London: CBCEW.

Charles, W. (2009) *Basil Hume: 10 Years On,* London: Burns and Oates.

Chenevix Trench, C. (1986) *The Frontier Scouts,* Oxford: Oxford University Press.

Clegg, S., Kornberger, M. and Pitsis, T. (2005) *Managing and Organisations: An Introduction to Theory and Practice,* London: SAGE.

Clement, S. and Ayers, D. (1976) *A Matrix of Organizational Leadership Dimensions,* Harrison, IN: United States Army Leadership Monograph Series, Monograph 8.

Clutterbuck, D. and Crainer, S. (1990) *Makers of Management,* London: Macmillan – now Palgrave Macmillan.

Collins, J. (2001) *Good to Great,* London: Random House.

Collins, J. (2009) *How The Mighty Fall,* London: Random House Business Books.

Collins, J. and Porras, J. (2000) *Built To Last: Successful Habits of Visionary Companies,* London: Random House Business Books.

Corrigan, P. (1999) *Shakespeare on Management: Leadership Lessons for Today's Managers,* London: Kogan Page.

Covey, S. (1992) *Principle-centred Leadership,* London: Simon and Schuster.

Covey, S.R. (2004) *The Eighth Habit: From Effectiveness to Greatness,* London: Simon and Schuster.

Coyte, M.E., Gilbert, P. and Nicholls, V. (eds.) (2007) *Spirituality, Values and Mental Health: Jewels for the Journey,* London: Jessica Kingsley.

Cunningham, I. (1999) *The Wisdom of Strategic Learning: The Self-Managed Learning Solution,* 2nd edn, Maidenhead: McGraw-Hill.

Cunningham, I., Bennett, D., and Dawes, G. (2000) *Self-Managed Learning in Action,* Aldershot: Gower.

Dalai Lama, The (2001) *The Art of Living,* London: Thorsons.

De Mello, A. (1988) *Walking on Water,* Dublin, Columba Press.

Department of Health (2001) *Learning from Bristol: The Report of The Public Inquiry into Children's Heart Surgery at the Bristol Royal Infirmary: 1984-1995* (Report by Sir Ian Kennedy QC), London: HMSO.

Department of Health (2007) *Putting People First,* London: DoH.

Department of Health (2008) *High Quality for All* (Lord Darzi's Report), London: DoH.

Drucker, P. (1967) *Managing for Results,* London: Heinemann.

Drucker, P. (1986) *The Frontiers of Management,* New York, NY: Khuman Talley Books.

Drucker, P. with Maciarello, J.A. (2008) *Greatness,* revised edn, London: Harper Business

Du Boulay, S. (1984) *Cicely Saunders: The Founder of the Modern Hospice Movement,* London: Hodder and Stoughton.

Edwards, R. and Townsend, H. (1965) *Business Enterprise: Its Growth and Organisation,* London: Macmillan - now Palgrave Macmillan.

Egan, G. (1986) *The Skilled Helper: A Model for Systematic Helping and Interpersonal Relating,* 5th edn, Monterey, CA: Brooks-Cole.

Eliot, G. (1964) *Middlemarch,* New York, NY: Signet (originally published in 1872).

Eliot. T.S. (1954) 'The Waste Land', in *Selected Poems,* London: Faber & Faber.

Ferguson, A. (2000) *Managing My Life,* London: Hodder and Stoughton.

Finkelstein, S. (2004) *Why Smart Executives Fail: And What Can You Learn From Their Mistakes,* New York, NY: Portfolio Books.

Fiornia, C. (2007) *Tough Choices: A Memoir,* Boston, MA: Nicholas Brealey

Flamholtz, E. and Randall, Y. (1989) *The Inner Game of Management*, London: Hutchinson.

Foresight Report (2008) *Mental Capital and Well-being*, London: Foresight.

Fowler, A. (1988) *Human Resource Management in Local Government*, London: Longman.

Fraser, D. (1994) *Nights Cross: A Life of Field Marshall Erwin Rommel*, London: HarperCollins.

Fry, T. (ed.) (1982) *The Rule of St Benedict in English*, Collegeiville, MN: The Liturgical Press.

Gardner, H. (1996) *Leading Minds: An Anatomy of Leadership*, London: HarperCollins.

George, B. (2003) *Authentic Leadership: Rediscovering the Secrets of Creating Lasting Value*, San Francisco, CA: Jossey-Bass.

Gilbert, P. (2005) *Leadership: Being Effective and Remaining Human,* Lyme Regis: Russell House Publishing.

Gilbert, P. (2009a) 'Leading to Well-being', in Thompson, N. and Bates, J. (eds) (2009)

Gilbert, P. (2009b) Interview with Bhai Sahib Dr Mohinder Singh, *The International Journal of Leadership in Public Services*, 5 (2).

Gilbert, P. (2010), *Social Work and Mental Health: The Value of Everything*, 2nd edn, Lyme Regis: Russell House Publishing.

Gilbert, P. and Scragg, T. (1992) *Managing to Care*, Sutton: Reed Business Publishing.

Giuliani, R.W. with Kurson, K. (2003) *Leadership*, London: Time Warner Paperbacks.

Glasby, J. and Peck, E. Ed. (2004) *Care Trusts: Partnership Working in Action*, Oxford: Radcliffe Press.

Goffee, R. and Jones, G. (2003) *The Character of a Corporation: How Your Company's Culture Can Make or Break your Business*, 2nd edn,London: Profile Books.

Goffee, R. and Jones, G. (2006) *Why Should Anyone Be Led By You?: What It Takes To Be An Authentic Leader*, Boston, MA: Harvard University Press.

Goldsmith, M. and Wharton, M. (1993) *Knowing Me, Knowing You: Exploring Personality Type and Temperament,* London: SPCK.

Goleman, D. (1996) *Emotional Intelligence,* London: Bloomsbury Publishing.

Goleman, D., Boyatzis, R. and McKee, A. (2002) *The New Leaders: Transforming the Art of Leadership into the Science of Results*, Boston, MA: Harvard Business School Press.

Grey-Thompson, T. (2001) *Seize the Day*, London: Hodder and Stoughton.

Haddon-Cave, C. QC (2009) *The Nimrod Review: An Independent Review into the Broader Issues Surrounding the Loss of the RAF Nimrod MR2 Aircraft XV230 in Afghanistan in 2006*, Report, London: The Stationery Office

Hampden-Turner, C. (1990) *Corporate Culture: From Vicious to Virtuous Circles*, London: Hutchinson Business.

Hampson, M. (2005) *Head Versus Heart – And Our Gut Reactions: The 21st Century Enneagram*, Ropley: O Books.

Handy, C. (1978) *Gods of Management,* London: Pan

Handy, C. (1989) *The Age of Unreason*, Boston, MA: Harvard Business School Press.

Harrison, R., and Stokes, H. (1990) *Diagnosing Organisation Culture*, Horsham: Roffey Park Management Institute.

Harvey-Jones, J. (1988) *Making It Happen: Reflections on Leadership*, London: Collins.

Hastings, M. (2008) *Nemesis: The Battle for Japan 1944-45*, London: Harper Perennial.

Healthcare Commission (2009) Investigation into Mid Staffordshire NHS Foundation Trust, London: Healthcare Commission.

Hebblethwaite, P. (1999) 'Obituary on Cardinal Hume', *The Guardian*, 18 June.

Hersey, P. (1984) *The Situational Leader*, New York, NY: Prentice-Hall.

Herzberg, F. (1960) *The Motivation to Work,* Chichester: John Wiley

Hick, S.F. (2009) *Mindfulness and Social Work*, Chicago, IL: Lyceum Books.

Hickey, M. (1992) *The Unforgettable Army*, Tunbridge Wells, Spellmount.

Holbeche, L. (2005) *The High Performance Organisation: Creating Dynamic Stability and Sustainable Success,* Oxford: Elseiver Butterworth-Heinemann.

Hollis, J. (2001) *Creating a Life: Finding your Individual Path*, Toronto, Canada: Inner City Books.

Horne, A. (1989) *MacMillan: 1957-1986*, London: Macmillan

Hunt, J.G. (1991) *Leadership: A New Synthesis*, London: SAGE.

Jamison, C. (2006) *Finding Sanctuary: Monastic Steps for Everyday Life*, London: Weidenfeld & Nicolson

Jenkins, S. (1995) *Accountable to None: The Tory Nationalisation of Britain*, London: Hamish Hamilton.

Johnson, G. and Scholes, K. (1989) *Exploring Corporate Strategy: Text and Cases,* London: Prentice-Hall.

Kaplan, R. and Norton, D. (1996) *The Balanced Scorecard: Translating Strategy into Action,* Boston, MA: Harvard Business School Press.

Keegan, J. (1987) *The Mask of Command*, New York, NY: Viking Penguin.

Keegan, J. (ed.) (1999) *Churchill's Generals*, London; Abacus.

Kelley, R. (1988) 'In Praise of Followers', *Harvard Business Review*, November/December 1988 .

Kennedy, Sir I. (2001) *Learning from Bristol: The Report of the Public Enquiry into Children's Heart Surgery at the Bristol Royal Infirmary 1984-1995,* London: The Stationery Office, CM5207

Kershaw, I. (1991) *Hitler*, Harlow: Longman.

Kershaw, I. (2009) *Hitler, the Germans, and the Final Solution,* New Haven, CT: Yale University Press.

Kilmann, R. (ed.) (1985) *Gaining Control of the Corporate Culture*, New York, NY: Jossey-Bass.

Kotter, J.P. (1988) *The Leadership Factor*, New York, NY: The Free Press.

Kotter, J.P. (1990) *A Force for Change: How Leadership Differs From Management*, New York, NY: The Free Press.

Kotter, J.P. (1996) *Leading Change*, Boston, MA: Havard Business School Press.

Kouzes, J. and Posner, B. (1990) *The Leadership Challenge*, San Francisco, CA: Jossey-Bass.

Kouzes, J. M. and Posner, B.Z. (2007) *The Leadership Challenge*, 4th edn, San Francisco, CA: Jossey-Bass.

Lao Tzu, (6th Century BC) *Tao Te Ching*. English version by Wilhelm, R. (1985) Harmondsworth: Penguin.

Leadbeater, C. (1999) *Living on Thin Air: The New Economy*, 2nd edn, London: Penguin Books.

Le Guin, U. (1977) *The Lathe of Heaven*, London: Gollancz.

Machiavelli, N. (1514, Penguin Edition 1961) *The Prince*, Harmondsworth: Penguin.

Mandela, N. (1994) *Long Walk to Freedom*, London: Little, Brown and Company.

Mannion, R., Davies, H.T.O. and Marshall, M.N. (2005) *Cultures for Performance in Health Care*, Maidenhead: Open University Press/McGraw-Hill Education.

Mant, A. (1984) *Leaders We Deserve*, London: Martin Robertson.

MacDonald Fraser, G. (1992) *Quartered Safe Out Here*, London: HarperCollins.

McGregor, D. (1960) *The Human Side of Enterprise*, New York, NY: McGraw-Hill.

McLean, A. and Marshall, J. (1988) *Cultures at Work*, London: LGMB.

Middleton, J. (2007) *Beyond Authority: Leadership in a Changing World,* Basingstoke: Palgrave Macmillan.

Midwinter, E. (1994) *The Development of Social Welfare in Britain*, Buckingham: Open University Press.

Miller, K., Walmsley, J. and Williams, S. (2007) Shared Leadership: An Idea Whose Time Has Come in Healthcare?, *The International Journal of Leadership in Public Services*, 3 (4).

Mintzberg, H. (1973) *The Nature of Managerial Work*, New York, NY: Harper and Row.

Morrell, M. and Capparell, S. (2001) *Shackleton's Way: Leadership Lessons From The Great Antarctic Explorer*, London: Nicholas Brealey.

Newman, J. (1996) *Shaping Organisational Cultures in Local Government,* London: Pitman.

NHS Confederation (2007) *The Challenges of Leadership in the NHS*, London: NHSC.

Nicholls, J. (1999) Value-centred Leadership: Applying Transforming Leadership to Produce Strategic Behaviour in Depth, Part 2, *Strategic Change* 8, November.

Norton-Taylor, R. and Rusbridger, A. (2001) I, Spy: Stella Rimington – Secrets Lies, *The Guardian, Weekend*, 8 September.

O'Hara, M. (2009) Voice of Experience, Interview with Dr Ian McPherson, *The Guardian, Society*, 24th June, p. 5.

Onyett, S (2009) The Keys to Unlock Leadership, *Health Service Journal*, 17th September, p. 24.

Ouchi, W. (1981) *Theory Z: How American Business Can Meet the Japanese Challenge*, Boston, MA: Addison-Wesley.

Palmer, H. (1995) *The Enneagram in Love and Work: Understanding Your Intimate and Business Relationships*, New York: HarperCollins.

Parikh, J. (1991) *Managing Yourself: Management by Detached Involvement*, Oxford: Blackwell.

Peters, T. (1989) *Thriving on Chaos*, London: Pan

Peters, T. and Austin, N. (1985) *A Passion for Excellence: The Leadership Difference*, Glasgow: William Collins.

Peters, T. and Waterman, R. (1982) *In Search of Excellence: Lessons from America's Best-run Companies*, New York, NY: HarperCollins.

Philpot, T. (1986) 'Values', in Philpot, T. Ed. (1986).

Philpot, T. (ed.) (1986) *Social Work: A Christian Perspective*, London: Lion

Philpot, T. (2001) Maureen Oswin, An Obituary, *The Guardian*, 17 July.

Pollock, J. (1985) *Shaftesbury The Reformer*, London: Hodder and Stoughton.

Rees, W. (1984) *The Skills of Management*, London: Crown Books.

Rimington, S. (2001) *Open Secret: From Bored Housewife to Head of the Secret Service*, London: Hutchinson.

Robinson, Sir G. (2007) *Foreword* in NHS Confederation (2007)Rolheiser, R. (1998) *Seeking Spirituality*, London: Hodder and Stoughton.

Rowe, D. (1998) *The Successful Self,* London: Fontana.

Sackmann, S. (1991) *Cultural Knowledge in Organisations*, London: SAGE

Schein, E. (2004) *Organisational Culture and Leadership*, Revised edn, San Francisco, CA: Jossey-Bass School Press.

Scragg, T. (2009) *Managing at the Front Line: A Handbook for Managers in Social Care*, 2nd edn, Brighton: OLM-Pavilion.

Scott, M.C. (2000) *Re-inspiring the Corporation*, Chichester: John Wiley.

Senge, P. (1990) *The Fifth Discipline: The Art & Practice of the Learning Organization*, New York, NY: Doubleday.

Skinner, K. (2010) Supervision, Management and Leadership, in Zwanenberg, Z.V. (ed.) (2010)

Small, H. (1998) *Florence Nightingale: Avenging Angel*, London: Constable.

Smith, P. and Peterson, M. (1988) *Leadership, Organisations and Culture*, London: SAGE

Spreckley, P. and Hart, T. (2001) Reigning Cats and Dogs, *The Health Service Journal*, 24 May.

Stewart, R. (1985), *The Reality of Management*, 2nd edn, London: William Heinemann.

Tannenbaum, R. and Schmidt, W. (1958) How to Choose a Leadership Pattern, Harvard Business Review, 36(2).

Thompson, N. (2009) *Tackling Bullying and Harassment in the Workplace: A Learning and Development Manual*, Lyme Regis: Russell House Publishing.

Thompson, N. and Bates, J. (eds) (2009) *Promoting Workplace Well-being*, Basingstoke: Palgrave Macmillan.

Van Zwanenberg, Z. (ed.) (2010) *Leadership in Social Care, Research Highlights 51*, London: Jessica Kingsley.

Webster, A. (2001) Embodied Leadership, *Ministry*, 2 (9).

Welch, J. with Byrne, J. (2001) *Jack: What I've Learned Leading a Great Company and Great People*, London: Headline Press.

Wheatley, M.J. (1999) *Leadership and the New Science: Discovering Order in a Chaotic World*, 2nd edn, San Francisco, CA: Berrett-Khoeler.

Wright, P.L. (1996) *Managerial Leadership*, London: Routledge

Wright, P.L and Taylor, D.S. (1994) *Improving Leadership Performance: Interpersonal Skills for Effective Leadership*, London: Prentice Hall

Yukl, G.A. (1994) *Leadership in Organisations*, revised edn, New Jersey, NJ: Prentice-Hall.

Biographies and Slides

Leadership Biographies

The examples presented here are meant to speak to a number of different professions and situations, but it is important to remember that 'Leadership' as a concept is by no means inextricably tied up with the famous. All of us have to, in the words of the song: 'Search for the hero inside ourselves'. There are likely to be examples of leadership within one's own family – and that is often where we look last! Some years after his father's death, one of the present authors (Peter) was reading a book on The Frontier Scouts, the old Indian Army's equivalent of the SAS and found references to his father's skills as a military trainer (Chenevix Trench, 1986, pp. 111 and 123).

Leaders don't always have responsibility for teams of people; sometimes they carry a torch for an ideal, a scientific discovery or a concept. Maureen Oswin, the winner of the *Community Care* magazine's award as the person who had made the greatest contribution to social care in the last 25 years, was exceptionally self-effacing but, due to her dogged efforts, at enormous cost to herself, the lives of disabled children were changed immeasurably for the better (see Atkinson, 2001 and Philpot, 2001).

Leaders very rarely achieve great things all by themselves, they have to inspire others to reach the goals. In the summation programme for the Spielberg television drama, 'Band of Brothers', one of the former American soldiers recalled his grandson asking him: 'Grandpa, were you a hero?'. 'No, son', he responded, 'But I served in a company of heroes' (BBC 2, 30 November 2001)

Nelson Mandela – Anti-apartheid Champion

Mandela, who opposed the apartheid regime in South Africa, was imprisoned for his beliefs, released in 1990, and was voted in as his country's first black President. He wrote about his experiences in the '*Long Walk to Freedom*' (Mandela, 1994) when he said:

> I was not born with a hunger to be free. I was born free – free in every way that I could know .... It was only when I began to learn that my boyhood freedom was an illusion, when I discovered as a young man that my freedom had already been taken from me, that I began to hunger for it. At first as a student, I wanted freedom only for myself ... but then I slowly saw that not only was I not free, but my brothers and sisters were not free. I saw that it was not just my freedom that was curtailed, but the freedom of everyone who looked like I did ... that is when .... the hunger for my own freedom became the greater hunger for the freedom of my people ... I am no more virtuous, self-sacrificing than the next man, but I found that I could not even enjoy the poor and limited freedoms I was allowed when I knew my people were not free. Freedom is indivisible; and the chains on any one of my people were the chains on all of them, the chains on all of my people were the chains on me.

Mandela's obvious qualities are:

• His integrity in holding firm to his beliefs; in willingness to sacrifice his personal happiness and comforts; and the forgiveness shown to his captors and political opponents.
• The formation and articulation of the vision for a new multiracial South Africa. His political opponent, ex-President de Klerk said of Mandela:

> The ordinary man would get to the top of the hill and sit down to admire the view. For Mandela there is always another peak to climb and another one after that. For the man of destiny the journey is never complete.

• The energy to take on the presidential role in his seventies and to tour other countries on behalf of South Africa.
• An extraordinary internal, personal process whereby justifiable anger is turned away from bitterness and into a search for connectedness over boundaries, and bring courage in sticking with the path he knew was right.
• His commitment to peace and justice, whereby Mandela uses his experience to urge other groups in conflict to find peace through justice.
• His ability to live the vision – for example, wearing the Springbok rugby jersey, with its Afrikaner connotations at the final of the Rugby World Cup, held in South Africa, and the mutual embrace with François Pienaar, the Afrikaner captain of the team.

Mandela, N. (1994) *Long Walk to Freedom,* London: Little, Brown and Company.

Florence Nightingale (1820–1910) – Founder of the Nursing Profession

At the height of her popularity, at the end of the Crimean War (1853–1856), Florence Nightingale was perceived by the British nation in highly visual, emotive and simplistic terms as: 'the lady with the lamp, (quoted in Small, 1998, p. 53), a comfort to injured and dying soldiers who had suffered immense hardship, not just at the hands of a resolute enemy and harsh climactic conditions, but through the incompetence and neglect of their own generals. Nightingale provided the human touch in a situation of great inhumanity, giving reassurance to people in a vulnerable state. A letter from a soldier gives a vivid example: 'What a comfort it was to see her pass. She would speak to one and nod and smile to many more …. We would kiss her shadow as it fell' (cited in Small, 1998, p. 53). I think we can all identify with the comfort that an experienced and reassuring presence brings when one is in a hospital ward.

In the years following her death in 1910, however, her legacy became much more clouded and complex. Biographies began to fit her into a socio-historical pattern as: a career woman appropriate to an era (1910–20) looking forward to female emancipation; or a victim of family tensions, a 1950s preoccupation.

What Small's biography draws out is Nightingale's searing honesty and self-appraisal which caused her profound distress when she realised that her Crimean War Hospital at Scutari had caused huge numbers of unnecessary deaths because of the lack of attention to basic hygiene. That realisation incapacitated her and then drove her forward relentlessly.

Nightingale's early life is marked by her dreams of heroic action, and very strong personal beliefs and self-belief. In her youth she visioned scenarios in which she achieved her goals. She felt guilty about this but, of course, nowadays personal development and sports coaches see visioning as a powerful tool for growth and achievement. Later, she spoke of: 'Infinite wisdom … wills mankind [*sic*] to create mankind by their own experience' (p. 14).

Bitterly frustrated at her role as a nineteenth century woman, she railed against her lot in life: 'Passion, intellect, moral activity, these three have never been satisfied in woman' (p. 11).

She was delighted, therefore, to be appointed, at the age of 32 as superintendent at a charitable hospital in Harley Street. Her ambition was wider, however, and she wished to be in a position to set up a nursing school in a large London teaching hospital, and advance nursing as a profession.

The commencement of the Crimean War, and *The Times* war correspondent's searing descriptions of an army betrayed by its 'leaders', led to the government sending Nightingale out to manage the nursing service. Arriving at the converted barracks at Scutari, her 'towering optimism and confidence' (p. 14), energy and administrative ability, coupled with an iron will created an organised regime, but one which was fatally under-mined by inadequate hygiene and battles with the medical staff.

While Nightingale's nurses put in place items conducive to human dignity, such as oper-ating screens and cared for those who were terminally ill.

> The army doctors, most of them young and very inexperienced, reacted to the horrors that surrounded them in different ways. The nurses found that even the kindly doctors became exasperated and unreasonable when the newly-arrived patients proved to be too far gone to recover. (p. 26)

Returning a national hero, Nightingale was honest enough to realise that the lack of basic hygiene precautions at her own hospital had naturally caused deaths which might have been prevented.

Minister, Sir Sidney Herbert, one of her main supporters in government, had set up a committee to raise money to establish a school of nursing at a major London teaching hospital. As Nightingale became more and more convinced that environmental, rather than individual, treatment was the key to good health, she distanced herself from the project for a time, but later became reconciled to it and played a major role in nurturing the development of a number of nurses she saw as future leaders – especially those in community settings.

In the twenty-first century, we have a stark irony of many parts of Britain's infrastructure: rail, water, public buildings crumbling in a way that Victorians would have found unimag-inable. The Health Service in the UK is still far too dominated by acute medicine as against primary and community care; and dominated by the image of the hospital and technological medicine, rather than environmental factors. Nightingale's prophetic ap-proach to public health is perhaps as important today as is her progenation of nursing as a profession. If she had been placed in charge of public health, at the highest point of her popularity and fame, rather than the environmentalist, Edwin Chadwick, who tended to alienate those he most needed to embrace, or Dr John Simon, the proponent of specific scientific advance rather than environmental factors, the health of the nation might be quite different today.

Small, H. (1998) *Florence Nightingale: Avenging Angel*, London: Constable.

Carly Fiorina – Business Person and Future US Politician?

Carly Fiorina was Chair and CEO of the computer giant, Hewlett Packard from 1999 to 2005. On her arrival from Lucent Technologies, she promised to shake up what she saw as a struggling culture and reinvent it as a company that made the Internet work for business and consumers. The Hewlett Packard website states that: 'Under her leadership, Hewlett Packard has returned to its roots of innovation and inventiveness, and is focused on delivering the best total customer experience'.

When William Hewlett and David Packard teamed up in 1938, it was pioneering work – Hewlett was said to provide the engineering brain and Packard the visible management in the workplace.

A mediaeval history and philosophy graduate, Carly Fiorina was 46 when she took over at Hewlett Packard. Revenue and earnings rose by 15 per cent at the end of her first year but then the Internet bubble imploded and sales were expected to fall by 10 per cent in this financial year before the terrorist attacks in the USA on 11 September 2001. The announcement of the HP/Compaq merger on 4 September 2001 was seen as something of a gamble, but Fiorina argued that: 'Doing this makes us a more effective competitor with a more effective market. For those who don't believe us – just watch!' (*The Guardian*, 5 September 2001).

During her time as CEO, Fiorina was known as:

- Highly energetic. She is said to rise at 4am and work out before heading into the office.
- Very communicative – and living the communications industry she worked in; customers and staff were able to email her direct.
- Having a conceptual framework which engages with the industry. In a talk on 13 November 2000, she commented:

> Looking at history, the Renaissance wasn't triggered by a single act of bravery or ingenuity. It was a collection of acts by individuals of many different talents. It was not fuelled by the bold acts of the few, but the everyday acts of many. The Digital Renaissance will be also.

- An ability to envision the future and to take calculated risks at a time of turbulence in the market. She makes the case that building sustainable value requires 'preserving the best and reinventing the rest'. Businesses need to look inward at how they are set up to adapt and create new value in this changing landscape, and look forward to find long-term opportunities for creating lasting value through change.

• The creation of a narrative for life. Returning to Stanford University where she graduated, Fiorina told students that they should: 'Begin the hard work of examining their lives to find out who they truly are'. To do that, she advised them to: treat fear as a motivator rather than an inhibitor, to make choices and decide to go forward rather than merely act out a role, and to actively engage in the process of distilling the 'text' of their lives down to its essence.

Jim Collins, in his book: *How The Mighty Fall* (2009) charts that, following the Hewlett-Packard acquisition of Compaq in 2001, the company's return on sales showed an erratic pattern. Fiorina's tenure came to an end on 7th February 2005. While opinions are mixed on her performance at Hewlett Packard, Collins states

> ... that Fiorina's tenure at HP ended in disappointed cannot be blamed entirely on her. In fact, Fiorina was exactly what the Board appears to have wanted: a charismatic, visionary leader who would bring the magnetic star power and passion for change needed to revolutionise the company.'

In Collins' estimation, HP was already in what he calls Stage 4: 'grasping for salvation', when an organisation 'reacts to a downturn by lurching for a silver bullet' (Collins, 2009, pp. 88-9).

Fiorina released her autobiography, *Tough Choices* in October 2006. Her comment on her loss of role at Hewlett-Packard was typically forthright:

> The worst thing I could have imagined happened. I lost my job in the most public way possible, and the press had a field day with it all over the world. And guess what? I'm still here. I am at peace and my soul is intact.

Since 2005, Carly Fiorina has had a number of business, media and academic roles, and has recently indicated that she would like to run for the United States Senate. In March 2009 she disclosed that she had been diagnosed with breast cancer and had undergone surgery with a good prognosis for a full recovery.

Perhaps her statement in June 2000 was prophetic. In talking about the journeys of life, Fiorina stated that:

> All you have to do is to engage your heart, your gut and your mind in every decision you make; engage your whole self and the journey will reveal itself with the passage of time (address to MIT, 2nd June 2000).

Collins, J. (2009) *How The Mighty Fall,* London: Random House Business Books.
The Guardian, 2001

Anthony Ashley-Cooper, Seventh Earl of Shaftesbury (1801-1885) – Social Reformer

It is difficult today to envisage an earl as the great champion of poor, disabled and dispossessed people over half a century of campaigning, but when Shaftesbury died, a vast crowd gathered outside Westminster Abbey, and his passing was mourned across the country in every sector of society. While most social reformers today, like sports people, are specialists in one area: child care, disability, employment, mental health and so on, Shaftesbury's indefatigable approach and immense sympathy for people deprived of decent opportunities in life meant that, as soon as he identified a challenge, he went into campaigning mode.

His successful campaigns to improve people's lives through legislative and community action were:

- Mental Health legislation, to introduce public care and commissioners to inspect asylums and people detained (Shaftesbury's commissioners still survive today as the Mental Health Act Commission).

- Curtailed the hours that children worked.

- Set up the Ragged Schools Union to educate children from poor families, and stopped inhumane practices such as children being used as chimney sweeps.

- The original foundation of the Union exists today as a modern charity – The Shaftesbury Society, working with people with disabilities in education and care services.

- Championed sound public health.

- Oversaw industrial reform in the Factory Acts.

- Encouraged Florence Nightingale, and badgered the Government to despatch a Sanitary Commission to the Crimean War zone.

- Played a part in bringing reforming and pastorally energetic bishops into the Church of England.

Shaftesbury demonstrated:

- An empathy with dispossessed people, which he turned into a compelling vision and then practical and enduring action.

- He had a strong personal faith which he lived and promoted as a driving force in his own life and social reforms.

• Despite personal tragedy and setbacks in his parliamentary programme, Shaftesbury showed a long-term commitment and he also used persuasion to win round die-hard opponents.

• The legislator always wanted to see for himself and experience, if possible, the people, the conditions he was determined to change, and to communicate directly with those who were oppressed by them. When he was bringing in legislation in the House of Commons to abolish the labour of children and women underground, he went down himself into a coalmine, not long after a number of people had been killed in a tragic pit shaft accident. When questioned by colleagues as to why he had gone down into the mine, he responded that he: 'thought it a duty: easier to talk after you have seen' (Pollock, 1985, p. 13).

• Shaftesbury had presence and was a passionate speaker.

• Integrity was a feature of his life. He was able to bridge the strong class divides in the 19th century and was instinctively trusted by a wide range of people. He used his own deeply unhappy childhood and his struggles with depression in a positive way so that his personal experience fuelled his social commitment and his empathy with dispossessed people, rather than turning him inwards on himself.

• Despite being profoundly serious about his beliefs and his reforming work, he had a well-developed sense of humour. Once he was booked to take the chair at a meeting of a charitable society and, through some mistake, nobody turned up but himself and one newspaper reporter. Getting up, he said: 'At this large and distinguished meeting ...'. The reporter looked up wonderingly. 'Why not?', said Shaftesbury, 'it's true. Am I not large, and are you not distinguished?!' Sharing a laugh at themselves, the two left the empty hall (Pollock, 1985, p. 165).

• Shaftesbury never forgot his core mission. When in meetings people started getting sidetracked, Shaftesbury would urge: 'What about the children?!' to bring them back to their mission (see Gilbert, 2010).

Gilbert, P. (2010), *Social Work and Mental Health: The Value of Everything*, 2nd edn, Lyme Regis: Russell House Publishing.
Pollock, J. (1985) *Shaftesbury The Reformer*, London: Hodder and Stoughton.

Ernest Shackleton – Explorer (1874-1922)

'The loyalty of your men [*sic*] is a sacred trust you carry', wrote Sir Ernest Shackleton, 'it is something which must never be betrayed, something which you must live up to' (cited in Morrell and Capparell, 2001, p. 215).

'He led, he did not drive' – G. Vibert Douglas, geologist, on the 'Quest' expedition (quoted in Morrell and Capparell, p. 104). Sir Ernest Shackleton, the Antarctic explorer, is now extensively used as a leadership model in business and military circles. Yet in many senses he was not a conventional success. As his recent biographers point out:

> He never led a group larger than twenty-seven, many of his expeditions were glorious 'failures' rather than conventional 'successes', and because of the advent of the first world war at the time of the 'Endurance' expedition to Antarctic (1914–1916), his fame was overshadowed for a long time. The 'Endurance' expedition is particularly noteworthy in that, having navigated through a thousand miles of icy waters, the ship became surrounded and trapped by ice just one day's sail from its destination. The expedition was stranded on the ice, unable to move; the ship was then crushed like a toy before their eyes; after camping on the ice the crew had to take to the lifeboats when the ice broke up, which saw them moving rapidly from four months of inactivity to an intense battle for survival that brought them to the limits of human capabilities. (p. 3)

Having reached Elephant Island, Shackleton took five men and sailed 800 miles in a lifeboat to reach the inhabited settlement on South Georgia. Even then there was a hazardous overland journey, made by Shackleton and two companions. And, once safe, Shackleton immediately turned round and joined the rescue party to save the majority of the crew marooned on Elephant Island. Every single member of the crew survived!

Shackleton's very singular leadership style is perhaps particularly apposite for leaders in the twenty-first century when rapid change and the need to manage that change effectively are endemic. Morrell and Capparell quote Richard Danzig, a past US Secretary of the Navy, as saying:

> The issue is not whether they [leaders] will encounter different types of crises; they will. The issue is whether or not they will change fast enough to be prepared for those crises when they occur. (p. 47)

Danzig praises the Shackleton model of leadership, and how it works on a number of levels:

• Leadership in response to danger and adversity;
• Working in extreme environments and surviving unforeseen challenges;
• Flexibility and planning; and
• Gaining and retaining the loyalty of those in your command.

Like many successful leaders, Danzig points to what he calls Shackleton's 'thoughtfulness': 'He was thoughtful in the emotional sense – he was empathetic and caring. He was also thoughtful in the cognitive sense – he thought logically even while under great stress.' (p. 47).

As another commentator on Shackleton's life and work, Eric Miller, Senior Advisor for an American investment bank, points out, Shackleton's methods and ideas about how to structure work are only now coming into their own as 'organisations have become more horizontal and less hierarchical' (p. 101, see also Scott, 2000, for his views on the changing nature of organisations).

Traditionally, Robert F. Scott – 'Scott of the Antarctic' – is the more famous explorer and, interestingly, while operating at the same time, and sometimes together, both men exemplified very different types of leadership. Morrell and Capparell quote Jeremy Larkem, Managing Director of OCTO, a crisis management company, as highlighting the differences between the two men:

> For Scott: ambitious, naïve technically, hierarchical, arrogant, wary of colleagues more able than himself, indifferent selector, poor trainer, bad safety record, gifted author ... For Shackleton, single-minded, excelled in crisis, technically sensible but not innovative, gregarious, excellent public speaker, broadly objective, good conceptual planner, effective selector and trainer, good safety record, erratic in business, bored by administration, politically astute. (p. 155)

Where Shackleton is an exemplar is that he had vision; planned meticulously for hazardous expeditions; held the strategic and the personal together; and was very incisive when crises arose. In addition, he had an ability to delegate but never shirked personal responsibility.

It is interesting that Shackleton's early life gave little sign of promise. He was introverted at an early age and achieved little at school. A schoolmaster who met Shackleton after he had become a famous explorer confessed: 'We never discovered you when you were at Dulwich'. 'No', Shackleton replied sympathetically, 'but I had not then discovered myself'! (p. 20).

Shackleton's family make-up is interesting. He grew up in a warm and supportive family environment with eight sisters and his grandmother and aunts also helping his mother with the children. Morrell and Capparell state that:

> It is no wonder that many people would later remark on his strong feminine sensibilities. Despite a burly physique, enormous stamina and a tough, no-nonsense manner, he could be nurturing and gentle, quick to forgive frailties and generous without seeking thanks in return. One friend called him 'a Viking with a mother's heart'. (p. 18)

The values of the family were founded on Quaker and Anglican approaches, and in later life Shackleton 'maintained his faith and his moral compass, balancing his contemplative, spiritual side with practical, humanistic commitment' (p. 19). The extraordinary feats that accompanied the 'Endurance' expedition brought forth a vivid feeling in Shackleton and his companions that 'Providence' had guided them. In the final march across the mountains and glaciers of South Georgia, it appeared to the three trekkers that they had a fourth companion with them. This was incorporated by T.S. Eliot in 'The Waste Land' (p. 187).

The biography by Morrell and Capparell is written as a narrative, but also has summaries at the end of each chapter which brings out the leadership lessons, which is most useful for trainers and students.

Some of Shackleton's main leadership attributes are as follows:

- Shackleton was strategic in his planning but paid close attention to detail.

- Shackleton was clear that, while he was determined to meet his goals, this must not be at the sacrifice of men's lives.

- Awareness of his environment was crucial in an explorer, and he always had in his mind a number of alternative courses of action so that his strategic approach was flexible, depending on the circumstances he encountered.

- As a leader, Shackleton was particularly good at identifying the right people for his expeditions and developing them.

- His choice of Frank Wild as his second in command was particularly insightful. Wild's complementary qualities were a vital element in safeguarding the welfare, and ultimately the lives, of the crew on the 'Endurance' expedition.

- It is clear that Shackleton made mistakes in human resource management in his first expeditions but he quickly learned from his mistakes.

- He was an expert in keeping up the morale of the crew. He encouraged celebrations, singing, games and so on. When only essentials could be taken on the boats after the Endurance sank in the ice, Shackleton insisted on the banjo being taken because 'it's vital, mental medicine and we shall need it' (p. 87).

- His biographers point out that he developed a personal relationship with each crew member, no matter what their rank or role. Dr Macklin, then a youngster at 24, said that, when Shackleton came across a member of the crew:

> he would get into conversation and talk to you in an intimate sort of way, asking you little things about yourself – how you were getting on, how you liked it, what particular side of the work you were enjoying most …

This communicativeness in Shackleton was one of the things his men valued in him. (p.117)

• Loyalty was one of Shackleton's prime requisites. He was loyal and he demanded it from his crew, and their loyalty to each other as well as to him. Shackleton also led by example, and lent a hand with even the most menial of tasks when that was required. This was not a dereliction of his strategic duty but a way of encouraging solidarity, getting to know the task and the people, and showing everybody how he wanted things done.

• Unlike many people, Shackleton was not jealous of other people's expertise. He hired and encouraged people who had better technical qualities than he did, and was keen to learn from them.

Eliot, T.S. (1954) 'The Waste Land' in *Selected Poems*, London: Faber & Faber/ Vibert-Douglas in Morrell, M. and Capparell, S. (2001) *Shackleton's Way: Leadership Lessons From The Great Antartic Explorer*, London: Nicholas Brealey.

Dame Tanni Grey-Thompson – Sports Person

Tanni Grey-Thompson is the former paralympic athlete who, born with spina bifida, and experiencing numerous setbacks in a sport not geared to her condition, turned herself into the most famous paralympian in the world.

At the time of the publication of her autobiography (*Seize the Day*, 2001) she had won the London Marathon five times and she brought home four gold medals from Sydney in the 2000 Olympics. Inadvertently she also brought disability issues into the spotlight when, on winning the 2000 Sports Personality of the Year Award at the BBC, the Corporation failed to provide a ramp so that she could join Denise Lewis and Steve Redgrave on the podium!

Grey-Thompson's motto for life is summed up in the first page of her book: 'I've never thought why me? I've never cried because I'm in a wheelchair and I've never felt bitter. This is just the way it is'. When her mother asked her what she thought about having spina bifida, she replied: 'Well, if it wasn't me then it would be someone else. I've got it, there's nothing I can do about it, so I might as well get on with it' (Grey-Thompson, 2001, p. 1). '*Seize the Day*' will speak to many people with disabilities and their families who have shown considerable leadership qualities in having to battle against the obstacles which society places in their paths. This autobiography looks at the difficulties the family experienced with doctors – for example, one suggesting that Tanni have a painful and lengthy operation to make her legs the same length. She challenged the doctor:

> I asked if the operation would do me any good and was told by a doctor, 'no, but your legs will be the same length'.
>
> 'But will I walk?'
>
> 'No, but your legs will be the same length'.
>
> I thought, no way. (p. 14)

Getting to a school that would suit her needs rather than the bureaucratic mind set of the Council, the difficulties in being taken seriously in her desire to be an athlete when she went to Loughborough University, and the exclusion of paralympic athletes at various international games, are detailed in a vivid, but very unpitying manner. Perhaps one of the most difficult times was when she had been extremely successful in Barcelona in 1992, winning four gold medals and breaking all four records, doing relatively less well at the Atlanta games, and being told by one official: 'You're finished now. You should retire'.

> Although 'a lot of coaches told me I failed ... I'm quite bloody-minded at times and I thought I'd carry on' (p. 132).

In the end, she won four gold medals in Sydney, continued a successful career in the London Marathon and became a Development Officer for the British Athletics Association. The extraordinary feat involved in both retaining a competitive edge over so many years, and being successful at distances ranging from 100 metres to the Marathon needs to be appreciated.

Some of the ingredients for Grey-Thompson's success are:

  • her lack of self-pity and her 'can do' philosophy. She clearly has enormous self-belief, and it is interesting to note that as a child, she didn't have idols like many young people do:

  > I didn't have posters of pop bands or film stars on my bedroom walls when I was growing up. I always wanted to be me, getting out there and doing something rather than just dreaming about it. (p. 31)

  • Clearly very competitive, and extremely focused, she also knows when to co-operate, and there is a description on pp.129-30 which most runners will appreciate where a competitor had pulled her through much of a marathon and, although she is feeling stronger at the finish, they go over the line together as that, in her own words, is 'fair'.

  • Her life has been centred around competing. In an amusing, but rather awe-inspiring anecdote, she admits that both she and her husband, Ian, would have been tempted to compete in a race on the morning of their wedding, if the race hadn't been cancelled!

  • A sense of humour is evident in all that she does and an ability to live life to the full.

  • She has the ability to make friendships which are mutually invigorating. Her friendship with the BBC presenter, Helen Rollason, who later died of cancer, but who was a great promoter of sport for people with disabilities, is particularly touching.

Tanni Grey-Thompson sums up her philosophy of life in the following words:

> What I do believe is that if you have the will, the luck, the time and the energy, you can achieve everything. Whether you can walk or not does not come into it. (p. 176)

Grey-Thompson, T. (2001) *Seize the Day*, London: Hodder and Stoughton.

Three Generals: Richard O'Connor, Erwin Rommel and 'Bill' Slim

Napoleon is said to have been overheard muttering: 'Don't give me good generals, give me lucky ones'! Both Richard O'Connor and Erwin Rommel were excellent generals, but the latter was fortunate that his tendency to lead from the front, while getting him into scrapes, never led to his capture – though it nearly did, while O'Connor was captured in North Africa and spent two years in a prisoner of war camp in Italy. Rommel is celebrated in books and films as a superb tactician and man who stood as an emblem against Nazism at the end of the war; while only the student of military history relishes O'Connor's nearly decisive North Africa Campaign in 1940/41.

O'Connor was slight of figure and mild of manner, but by the time he faced the Italian invasion of the western desert in September 1940, he had already endured battles in the Alpine snows, the mud of Ypres and on the north-west frontier of India. During World War I he received a DSO and Bar, an MC and the Italian Silver Medal for Valour.

In September 1940, O'Connor commanded 36,000 British and commonwealth troops against 80,000 Italians, but he had trained his soldiers to a high degree of battle-readiness, he had the edge in equipment and the intelligence to exploit it. First, using 'Fabian' tactics – drawing the enemy onto ground of his own choosing, he then turned on them and conducted a lightning campaign which resulted in the complete capitulation of a large Italian army and its allies. 35,000 officers and men had advanced 500 miles in ten weeks in vehicles which were in a poor state of repair before the advance started. Over 130,000 Italian and Libyan soldiers had been taken prisoner, 180 medium and about 200 light tanks, 845 guns and an immense amount of other material were captured (Keegan, 1999). Pitt, the author of the chapter on O'Connor in this edited work, quotes the general as saying: 'I think this may be termed a complete victory as none of the enemy escaped' (p. 197). This was the kind of wholesale victory, very rarely accomplished by British generals in World Wars I or II. O'Connor's victory was truly the British blitzkrieg.

How did he achieve this astonishing feat? He did it by:

> • Meticulous planning – with exercises conducted both on paper and on specially constructed outdoor sites.

> • By retaining the element of surprise and an extraordinary degree of masking his intentions so as to confuse the enemy. The Italians seemed to be constantly surprised by the rapidity of O'Connor's movement and the direction from which his troops came. He also managed to build up an image in the Italians' minds that they were outnumbered by O'Connor, rather than outnumbering him by more than two to one!

> • He concentrated initially on gaining air supremacy.

• O'Connor had superior equipment, but that does not necessarily lead to victory in itself. Sometimes excellent equipment is used inappropriately – for example, the use of tanks in penny packets (small groups) rather than to punch through the enemy's lines.

• O'Connor understood his technology and used it skilfully.

• Speed of thought and action.

• Pitt remarks on O'Connor 'closely attending all phases of the day's actions' (p. 190). This Wellingtonian concept of attention to the process of the strategy, while trusting junior commanders and allowing them to show initiative, is a constant theme in successful generalship.

• Calculated risk taking was demonstrated when, rather than simply securing ground gained, which was a British flaw in the two world wars, O'Connor constantly urged his troops forward in swinging hooks to cut off his opponents.

• To push soldiers who were tired, thirsty, battle weary and whose vehicles were almost past repair, required a high degree of motivation, morale and trust. O'Connor's men trusted him and his leadership competence. The Australian advance along the coast, through minefields and immensely difficult terrain ensured that the northern arm of O'Connor's pincer movement trapped the Italian rearguard and pushed them into the arms of other forces. Australian troops had a certain in-built distrust of British commanders, but Pitt remarks on their trust for O'Connor.

North Africa was very nearly captured in its entirety. If it had been, then Rommel's campaign in the western desert would never have materialised, because it would not have been possible, and the war would have been shortened immeasurably. Unfortunately, other strategic requirements – in the end mistaken ones – meant that the majority of O'Connor's force were withdrawn. O'Connor was very unluckily captured by forward troops of Rommel's command. He spent two years in a prison of war camp, and enterprisingly escaped wearing clothes from the drama company! He later played a distinguished role in the battle for Normandy.

O'Connor is little known today. If he hadn't been captured and had pressed on, then the history of the Second World War might have been very different. As Pitt remarks:

The ifs of history are of course imponderable. But one certainty is that the loss, so early, of Richard Nugent O'Connor from the higher direction of Britain's war effort was as unfortunate for us as it was for him. (Keegan, 1991, p. 198)

James Mason in the film, 'Desert Fox', and the depiction of him in 'The Longest Day' have etched the image of Erwin Rommel on our memories as the consummate commander; the creator of the Africa Corps; the 'Good German' who won the respect of his adversaries; the honourable man whom Hitler forced to his death as the Führer's paranoia grew. Winston Churchill himself referred to Rommel in the House of Commons, paying tribute to 'a very daring and skilful opponent ... and, may I say across the havoc of war, a great general' (quoted in Fraser, 1994, p. 5).

Fraser, a former soldier as well as an historian, highlights three qualities which, when combined, composed the battlefield commander's skill:

1. *Temperament* The commander relishes the challenges. This does not mean that he or she is unaware or uncaring about the human cost, but relishes the adrenaline of the crisis.

2. *An understanding of the history, knowledge base and skills of war*
The great commanders have an ability to carry technical and professional expertise in their head and apply it in a variety of situations with practical skill and a sense of what will work, when and why. It was this sense which men in the Africa Corps called Rommel's 'Fingerspitzengefuhl' – 'his almost animal response to the dangers, the chances, the currents of battle' (Fraser, 1994, p. 7).

3. *The ability to think and act with clarity, with resolution and with speed*
This was an attribute that O'Connor and Rommel shared. They were attributes which the British Army had honed in the relatively small colonial wars, but appeared to have difficulty in the world wars in translating this to larger theatres. The Germans had the immense advantage that they had garnered their most able people and put them through a staff college training which enabled them to ingest and then use those skills in a variety of theatres of war during 1939 to 1945.

Rommel had a number of other attributes:

1. Fraser makes a major point about Rommel's integrity and loyalty. Rommel wrote that once a commander had won his soldiers' trust, they 'will follow him through thick and thin' (p. 39). The Field Marshal's loyalty to his country, its leaders (mistaken until the veil was lifted from his eyes), his family, his staff and his men was, in Fraser's words, 'wholly faithful, wholly true' (p. 19). Rommel did not always find that loyalty returned and, towards the end of his time in Africa, the lack of trust by his superiors in Berlin caused him both personal and professional unhappiness and also took the edge off his military competence: 'professionally, Rommel was deeply unhappy. It seemed to him that his opinion on military essentials had recently been disregarded or overruled. He felt that he was no longer trusted' (p. 402).

2. Rommel had instinctive leadership qualities which rarely seemed to falter: strategic grasp, clarity of thinking, incisiveness, and speed of thought and action. While leading the point of the German blitzkrieg through France in 1940, he moved so fast that his unit was called the Gespensterdivision – 'the ghost

division'. Rommel 'remained absolutely convinced that in mobile operations a commander must influence decision at the critical point. In an advance, this is at the tip of the spear' (p. 207).

3. Related to this he exercised dynamic action at critical points. Rommel believed that: 'in a fluid battle situation, near superhuman energy is required at particular places and particular moments; and that the function of the commander is to supply that energy where it is even temporarily defective'. Through this he imposed his will and imprinted his image on his adversaries in a manner reminiscent of other great commanders.

4. Certainly, there has been controversy around Rommel's military judgement in certain instances. At times he appears to have been reckless in his command in the western desert, and Fraser believes that an extremely competent staff group sometimes got their general out of trouble. The German military machine was one of the most efficient of this or any other age, and sometimes Rommel appears to have ridden it too hard. Rommel's justification was that the margins of victory and defeat in Africa were very slim, and just as in O'Connor's campaign, it was sometimes right to push for outright victory. In Normandy, the controversy still rages as to whether Rommel's dictum of fight the allies on the beaches, or Von Rundstedt's concept of a mobile strike force of panzers. In the event, it looks likely that Rommel was right. Allied air power was such that, unless the allies were stopped on the beaches, which they very nearly were in parts of the American sector, the allies would have overwhelming strength to move through France.

5. Rommel was well known for his sense of humour and also his chivalry. He recognised the talents of his adversaries, carrying a copy of Wavell's published essays on generalship with him on campaign. When a British commando was captured and taken to Rommel, the Field Marshal didn't use the obvious trick of waiting for the officer to come to him at his desk, but moved forward to meet him, shake him by the hands and entered into an animated discussion.

6. Above all, Rommel allied the strategic with the human: 'he thought ahead with clarity, he had a vision, a concept of battle before he launched it. And he shared it with his subordinates, he put men in his mind. This was far superior to attempting to preordain their every action' (Fraser, p. 418).

William ('Uncle Bill') Slim

Slim's 14th army in Burma was sometimes referred to as 'the forgotten army'. William Slim might also have been referred to as the forgotten general in the years immediately after the war: an unfashionable early career with the Gurkha Rifles, and an unspectacular start to the war, it was Slim who had halted the Japanese invasion at the gates of India, in the desperately fought battles of Kohima and Imphal, and then, having rebuilt an army, he launched it against the Japanese in a campaign that took the allies back through Burma. It was apt that Slim's own account of the campaign should have been called 'defeat into victory'. Both sides in the war used a great deal of propaganda, and it is useful to get behind that to see the man beneath the general's hat. As the author, George MacDonald Fraser wrote in his autobiography of life as a private soldier in the Burma Campaign: 'Quartered Safe Out Here' (1992):

> By rights each official work should have a companion volume in which the lowliest actor gives his version (like Sydenham Pointz for the Thirty Years War or Rifleman Harris in the Peninsula); it would at least give posterity a sense of perspective. (p. xi)

Lord Louis Mountbatten, Supreme Commander, south-east Asia, stated firmly that 'Slim was the finest general the second world war produced' (Fraser, 1992, p. 31), but perhaps the frontline soldier's perspective is even more crucial, especially in fighting that often became hand-to-hand combat:

> The biggest boost to morale was the burly man who came to talk to the assem bled battalion by the lake shore – I'm not sure when, but it was unforgettable. Slim was like that: the only man I've ever seen who had a force that came out of him, a strength of personality that I have puzzled over since, for there was no apparent reason for it … His appearance was plain enough: large, heavily built, grim faced … the rakish Gurkha that was at odds with the slung carbine … he might have been a yard foreman who had become a managing director … nor was he an orator.

• Slim had that ability to be 'Uncle Bill', the soldier's trusted uncle, while at no time there being any doubt who was in command.

• Duncan Anderson who wrote the chapter on Slim in Keegan's edited work says that Field Marshall Slim 'revealed a natural talent as a manager of men' (1992, p. 302). Bill Slim would often pick out people who seemed to be rogues or misfits and bring out the best of them. At his time with the Ghurkhas, he learned the languages and customs of the people of north India. The 14th Army, in Hickey's (1992) opinion was possibly the most multiracial army since those of the ancient world, and he brought the best out of a potentially complex and difficult command.

• Because of the particular difficulties in Burma, Slim never forgot the importance of good logistics and took great care to see that his staff officers knew that their contribution had a vital role to play in success at the front line.

• 'Slim was both a good student and a good teacher' (1991, p. 303). He could absorb both quantity and quality of information and impart it well.

• Slim always accepted responsibility. The retreat from Burma was handled with great determination and skill.

• Because of the massive defeat the army had suffered and its heterogeneous nature, Slim decided not only to train his troops but to motivate them by personal contact.

• 'From past experience, Slim had learned that the best approach was the most simple and direct – to talk to as many troops as he could, man to man, cutting through the traditional barriers of military hierarchy' (p. 313 – a method which Fraser describes so graphically).

• Some generals are characterised, sometimes unfairly, as either good at defence or offence. Slim was a master of both, and Anderson believes that he ranks with Guderian, Manstein and Patton as an offensive commander (p. 319).

It was a desperately hard campaign and there still remains the memorial to the defence at Kohima and Imphal:

When you go home, tell them of us and say
For your tomorrow we gave our today.
(quoted in Hickey, 1992, p. 263)

Anderson, D. 'Slim' in Keegan, J (ed.) (2005).
Fraser, D. (1994) *Nights Cross: A Life of Field Marshall Erwin Rommel*, London: HarperCollins.
Hickey, M. (1992) *The Unforgettable Army*, Tunbridge Wells, Spellmount.
Keegan, J. (ed.) (2005) *Churchill's Generals*, London: Cassell Military Paperbacks.
MacDonald Fraser G. (1992) *Quartered Safe Out Here*, London: HarperCollins.
Pitt, B. 'O'Connor' in Keegan, J. (ed.) (2005)

Dame Stella Rimington – Spy Supremo

When the James Bond films introduced the admirable Dame Judi Dench as the new 'M', the Head of the British Secret Service, it was either art imitating life, or perhaps life imitating art?! In 1993, Stella Rimington became the first female Head of MI5, and the first Head of the Secret Service to be named and photographed.

She was also the first Secret Service Chief to publish her memoirs, and it was then that she hit a storm of criticism and accusations of double standards because of the strong grip that MI5 had kept over revelations by its operatives (see Rimington, 2001, and Norton-Taylor and Rusbridger, 2001).

Rimington's is a quite extraordinary career story, and yet, perhaps because of a natural reticence of working in such a secretive and secret organisation, or perhaps because of the rigour of the censorship which she submitted to, Stella Rimington's leadership characteristics remain amazingly opaque. Born in Essex, educated at Nottingham High School, and with her first job as assistant archivist in Worcestershire County Records Office, there was nothing apparent to foretell her meteoric rise when, in 1967, she was approached by the MI5 representative in India and asked if she would like to do some work on a temporary basis.

On her return to the UK in 1969, she joined MI5 on a permanent basis but:

> it soon became clear that a strict sex discrimination policy was in place at MI5. It did not matter that I had a degree ... the policy was that men were recruited as what were called 'officers' and women had their own career structure, a second-class career as 'assistant officers'. (Rimington, 2001, p. 5)

As Norton-Taylor and Rusbridger (2001, p. 18) point out:

> It is difficult to imagine anyone rising to the top of the pile without a streak of ruthlessness to match whatever analytical or managerial qualities they might also have. And yet, whether due to modesty, a gift for understatement, or the work of the Whitehall censor – the book itself does not quite explain the meteoric career of this woman.

Perhaps one reason is the state of MI5 which Rimington describes.

She is affectionately scathing of a number of the operatives, usually people who have been successful in a military career, but now either damaged or out of their depth. She also sardonically remarks that one of the best sources of information about the communist party of Great Britain was the Morning Star newspaper. Rimington opines that the large standing order for the newspaper from MI5 may well have kept that newspaper going when otherwise it might have folded!

Rimington pushed to become a full officer of MI5, clearly causing great consternation amongst the tweed suits(!) and, in 1973, was so promoted. By the late 1970s, and now with two children at home, she was looking to break through the glass ceiling to try and move into the job of agent-running. Already Rimington was just demonstrating attributes of high intelligence, perception of situations and immense determination to succeed in an inimical environment.

Determination was required in great measure when her spell as an agent-runner coincided with her two daughters being both of school age. In one instance, she was due to meet an agent who was considering defecting and had agreed to meet him in a safe house in the Barbican. Just as she was due to set off, she was phoned to say that her younger daughter had been taken ill and rushed to St Bartholomew's Hospital. Torn between abandoning her daughter or the agent she was due to meet, she managed to fulfil both obligations by going via the safe house to St Bartholomew's Hospital and borrowing money from the would-be defector to pay for the taxi involved in this complex manoeuvre. Rimington speculates whether the apparent scarcity of funds available to MI5 operatives had any influence on the prospective defector's decision, but eventually he decided not to cross the line!

Rimington acknowledges that her frequent absences on operations and the stresses inherent in her work caused tension in her marriage and the couple separated. When, in 1986, she was promoted to Director of Counter Espionage (or 'K', as it was known then) she was still caring for her two daughters, then aged 12 and 16, although her book gives some detail of the tensions of the job – for example, the Georgi Markov assassination and the IRA bombing campaign in London, that and its effect on the family, one presumes that all this was fairly much downplayed.

When asked by Norton-Taylor and Rusbridger about what qualities and techniques she had and used, Rimington talks about the theme of her book which is very much about being a woman in a man's world, and a very ultraconservative world at that. She talks to the journalist about the advantages of gender: 'Any woman will tell you, you work out what you can use to your advantage, that fact that you're female – and that's what you do' (Norton-Taylor and Rusbridger, 2001, p. 18).

Rimington felt that the very male-dominated environment which made it so difficult for her to progress also left her colleagues very unused to coping with a woman who was both intelligent and decisive - perhaps something akin to the difficulties that Margaret Thatcher's Cabinet had in coping with her (Blake, 1997).

Rimington certainly had to display steel in mind and spirit and, as she says:

> I've never been one to retreat at the first whiff of gunshot (about the pressure on her when she wanted to publish her memoirs). If you terrorise everybody who wishes to say anything – even like me, originally, wanting to write about what it's like being a woman through the period I've been working – then clearly

people won't use the system, and that would be a pity. What you need is a system people are encouraged to use. (cited in Norton-Taylor and Rusbridger, 2001, p. 21)

Perhaps in the Security Services more than anywhere there are the issues of ethical engagement, and the need to balance ends and means:

> The agent-running thing does bring you up sharp with the ethical dilemma of asking people to do things that might put them at risk. And that is the moment, when it's personalised and you're dealing with people face-to-face, that you actually focus on. (p. 22)

Rimington still sees herself as fighting these battles, in a new life in the boardroom of British companies – still arguing for diversity and for talent to be recognised in whatever form:

> By the time I left public service, I think it's true to say that women were regarded as paid-up members of the human race. But in the boardrooms of British companies, that really is not yet the case. (p. 29)

Blake, R. (1997) *The Conservative Party from Peel to Churchill*, London: Arrow Books.
Norton-Taylor, R. and Rusbridger, A. (2001) I, Spy: Stella Rimington – Secrets Lies, *The Guardian, Weekend*, 8 September.
Rimington, S. (2001) *Open Secret: From Bored Housewife to Head of the Secret Service*, London: Hutchinson.

Sir Alex Ferguson – Football Manager

> On one of my more philosophical days, I tried to define the feeling that should exist among footballers aspiring to reach the heights: 'when you can look round this dressing room and be glad that you have every player you see will be out there shoulder-to-shoulder with you, then you will know you really do have a team'. (Ferguson, 2000, p. 255)

Even enemies of Manchester United, and there are many, would have to admit that the club has had a remarkably successful run: Premier League championships, including two domestic league and cup doubles, and the unique treble of 1999, the European Championship again in 2008 and the World Club championship in 2000 and 2008, while playing attractive, attacking football.

Most of the revival of this open 'sleeping giant' of a football club must be down to the skill and sheer will power of the rugged Scot from the Govan district of Glasgow who also temporarily disrupted the hegemony of Rangers and Celtic in the Scottish Premier League, when he led unfancied Aberdeen to four championships.

Perhaps the first attribute to strike one about Ferguson is his loyalty to kith and kin. Born and brought up in a tough, Clydeside area of Glasgow, his comments about his family are always warm, sometimes moving: 'Nobody", he writes, "could have had a better home than I had' (p. 11).

His father was demanding but supportive of his ambitions, and his mother was always a staunch figure backing him. Loyalty is a major ingredient in Ferguson's make-up. He expresses this about his family, his Govan friends, many of the managers and chairmen he worked with and for, and players such as Bryan Robson and Steve Bruce, captains during his time at United.

He has absolutely no time for dishonesty or lack of integrity, and is caustic in his comments:

> The club [Falkirk] had suffered a grievous loss when Willy Palmer ceased to be chairman. He was a man who could be trusted, which is something I never felt able to say about his successor. (p. 119)

When parting from Falkirk FC, Ferguson comments that the manager 'found it difficult to look me in the eye', (yes, I'm sure many of us have experienced that!). But Ferguson has his revenge, and has no problem delighting in it: 'When they (Falkirk) came calling on my next employers, Ayr United, I scored the winning goal against Prentice's team. One good team deserves another!' (p. 122).

Sir Alex is realistic about people, but can also be generous about their good qualities. In writing about the effervescent but somewhat erratic former Scotland Manager, Ally MacLeod, he writes: 'Some might have been put off by the dream factory Ally carried in his head but I was stimulated by his bubbling enthusiasm' (p. 123).

Although Ferguson may be seen as the finished product today, he studied those around him – for example:

> There was much to be learned on that course at Lilleshall and the star of the show for me was Jimmy Sirrell … It was instantly obvious that he commanded the respect of everybody at Lilleshall and I've decided that I wouldn't neglect any opportunity to listen to him. He did not disappoint me. The principles of management he laid down with such emphasis were often simple but their importance was so undeniable that I always tried to adhere to them … It was a reminder that commonsense, when there is enough of it, amounts to wisdom. (p. 121)

The Celtic and Scotland Manager, Jock Stein, was perhaps his main mentor. In this he tells stories against himself which shows a capacity for humility and willingness to learn which is very instructive. When Ferguson passes some minors campaigning for strike funds without contributing, Stein calls him back with the words:

'I'm surprised at you of all people forgetting these lads'. I offered no apology or excuse. It was an important message he was giving me and I have never forgotten it. In fact, I go out of my way if I ever see anyone in that position or selling the Big Issue.

For those of us who are, or have been, in senior leadership positions, Sir Alex's experience at Manchester United is encouraging in a paradoxical way. He was not an instant success, far from it. There are strong indications that, if he had not won a particularly crucial cup game in his third full season at the club, Ferguson might well have been sacked and regarded as 'a failure'. Sir Alex came into potentially the world's biggest football club as a man who had transformed Scottish football through his success with Aberdeen, but it took six full seasons to bring the championship to Old Trafford.

It is primarily to his mother that Ferguson attributes his courage and determination (p. 244), and he is quite clear about his desire to build long-standing success on firm foundations, even when the sky was darkest:

> My aim in management has always been to lay foundations that will make a club successful for years, or even decades. Flash-in-the-pan achievements, such as some good runs in cup competitions … could never satisfy me … putting them in a position to challenge consistently would, I knew, be a long haul. I would have to build from the bottom up, rectifying the flaws I had recognised and spreading my influence and self-belief through every layer of the organisation. (p. 242)

It is useful to look at a modern management tool like the Balanced Scorecard when considering Ferguson's achievements at United, and the tensions between the need for instant success against long-term success, financial returns against the building of a team able to compete at the highest level, and a learning process which builds on success and continues it.

The Balanced Scorecard (see Kaplan and Norton, 1996) has performance measures under four headings:

- The business process perspective – is the organisation producing what it needs?

- The financial perspective – is the organisation operating efficiently and within budget?

- The learning perspective – does the organisation develop its staff, and take on board developments in technology?

- The customer perspective – how does the organisation's customers perceive it? Is the organisation satisfying its main customers?

Ferguson has probably never read the book but he has in effect achieved 'strategic alignment' from the top to the bottom of the organisation which is what the Balance Scorecard proposes, a performance method promoted by the Audit Commission and Cabinet Office (2001). One leadership factor which comes out most frequently is his attention to people: their potential, their vital contribution to the whole, their individual needs - whether it be his young stars, possible future players, stars in temporary disgrace (for example, Eric Cantona), and indeed everybody in the organisation:

> I wanted to form a personal link with everybody around the place – not just the players, the coaches and the backroom staff – but the office workers, the cooks and servers in the canteen and the laundry ladies. All had to believe that they were part of the club and that a resurgence was coming. (p. 242)

Ferguson believes everybody has a vital part to play in a sophisticated modern organisation. With that, however, is a willingness to make the tough decisions. Manchester United in 1986, when he took over, had a drinking culture: 'Drinking to Failure' (p. 239) as he calls it, and Ferguson ruthlessly confronted it, rid the club of those he felt were undermining its success, and after a disappointing 1994/95 season, sold Paul Ince ('the decision to sell Paul Ince was mine alone and nobody at Old Trafford was inclined to let me forget the fact', p. 361) and two other key players and won the double with the team of 'kids', as the football commentator, Alan Hansen, termed them. Ferguson's ruthlessness at the beginning of the season earned him a great deal of opprobrium and, as he puts it: 'there was nothing splendid about my isolation' (p. 361) but Sir Alex had the strength of character to ride that temporary unpopularity.

Scouting for talent, setting up a football academy and encouraging his young players, has produced a crop of youngsters: Beckham, Giggs, Scholes and so on, who are almost priceless. Again, Ferguson pays tribute to past mentors:

He had a good way with young players and always made you feel special. Remembering how much that meant to me then, I have tried hard to convey warmth and reassurance to youngsters I have dealt with as a manager (p. 30)

Throughout the book, there is a demonstration of an immense mental strength, but not in any sense an insensitivity. This is an emotional man who allows, what I will term his emotional dialogue to convey a passion for people, for the game and for life.

There is considerable misunderstanding about the emotional content in leadership. The 'Iron Duke' Wellington himself, had iron will and self-control in times of conflict, but was moved to tears at the cost afterwards. Following the Battle of Waterloo, a friend recalls:

His eye glistening and his voice broken as he spoke of the losses sustained at Waterloo, he said, 'I hope to God I have fought my last battle ... while I am in the thick of it I am too much occupied to feel anything; but it is wretched just after .... and I always say that next to a battle lost, the greatest misery is a battle gained' (quoted in Keegan, 1987, p. 161)

A sense of humour shines through Ferguson's book, as does a very clear sense of integrity and what is right and wrong – old-fashioned terms maybe, but something, coupled with a Wellingtonian attentiveness to any situation, are qualities his players clearly respond to.

Ferguson, A. (2000) *Managing My Life*, London: Hodder and Stoughton.
Holbeche, L. (2005) *The High Performance Organisation: Creating Dynamic Stability and Sustainable Success*, Oxford: Elseiver Butterworth-Heinemann.
Kaplan, R. and Norton, D. (1996) *The Balanced Scorecard: Translating Strategy into Action,* Boston, MA: Harvard Business School Press.
Keegan, J. (1987) *The Mask of Command*, New York, NY: Viking Penguin.

Jack Welch – Business Person

Bennis (1989) quotes Jack Welch, retired Chief Executive of General Electric, as saying:

> Yesterday's idea of the boss, who became the boss because he or she knew one more fact than the person working for them, is yesterday's manager. Tomorrow's person leads through a vision, a shared set of values, a shared objective. (p. 194)

Welch is one of the most quoted examples of corporate business leaders in the 20th century, leading General Electric, at times a major challenge, and making it a world leader through initiatives like Six SIGMA Quality, Globalisation and E-Business. In his book: *Good to Great* (2001), Jim Collins points to General Electric as a company which grows its leaders who, in turn, are committed to the creation of something greater and longer-lasting than their own egos. To achieve this, they need a deeper understanding of the company's purpose and possibilities than is often achieved by bringing in a high-profile outsider.

In his autobiography (Welch with Byrne, 2001), Welch interestingly is very clear to acknowledge other people rather than point to his own ego, though there is also no doubt concerning the man's self-belief. As he puts it:

> At every moment of my life, I've been lucky to have people at my side whose support, encouragement and love made all the difference in the world. They filled my journey with great fun and learning. They often made me look better than I am. (p. 439)

Welch also highlights an issue which will be true of a number of great leaders. While a number, in the Napoleonic mode are clearly well ahead of most of their contemporaries, the talent in others is to bring out the very best of those around them. Welch puts it very graphically:

> I sometimes said that while I might not be the brightest bulb in the chandelier, over the years I've always thought I was pretty good at getting most of the bulbs to light up. (ibid.)

In a chapter entitled 'What this CEO thing is all about', Welch sets out 'some of the ideas that worked for me'. The ones he names are:

• *Integrity* Welch recounts that he was once asked:

'   How can you be a good Catholic and a business man at the same time?'

Welch says that he answered: 'Emphatically, "I am"'.

The simple answer is: by maintaining integrity, establishing it and never wavering from it supported everything I did through good and bad times. People may not have agreed with me on every issue – and I may not have been right all the time – but they always knew they were getting it straight and honest .... I never had two agendas. There was only one way – the straight way'. (p. 381)

• *The Corporation and the community* Social responsibility begins with a company that is strong in itself and willing and able to operate responsibly, and invest in people and the community.

• *Setting a tone* 'The organisation takes its cue from the person on top. I always told our business leaders their intensity determined their organisation intensity. The CEO sets the tone. Every day, I try to get into the scheme of every person in the place. I wanted them to feel my presence' (p. 382). This, as many of us know, is a highly ambitious aspiration in a large organisation. If you read Keegan (1987) you will see that Alexander the Great took this approach, but of course it was in a relatively small army on a foreign expedition, and therefore pulled very tightly together through circumstances in a way which enabled Alexander to exert his formidable personality to its maximum extent. Keegan describes Alexander in battle:

> The knowledge that their King was taking the supreme risk drove capable and well-briefed subordinates, at the head of drilled and self-confident troops, to fight as hard and skilfully *as if he had been at the elbow of each one of them*. (p. 81, emphasis added)

Welch, however, clearly had considerable success in creating this person alignment.

• *In maximising an organisation's intellect* This is what Welch calls: 'getting every employee's mind into the game', and GE worked hard at garnering, learning from all parts of the organisation so as to gain competitive advantage.

• *People first, strategy second* Welch found that the company had some excellent strategies but performance was mediocre and failed to meet customer requirements until the right people were brought into place.

• *Informality* By this, Welch means cutting down on bureaucracy, welcoming ideas and including people so that: 'it's about making sure everybody counts – and everybody knows they count' (p. 384).

• *Self-confidence* Welch believes that arrogance 'is a killer' and so is 'wearing ambition on one's sleeve'. On the other hand, insecure people find it difficult to be challenged and are usually thrown badly off balance by proposals for change. Welch advises 'seeking out people who are comfortable in their own skin' (p. 384).

He also advises: 'Don't ever compromise "being you" for any damn job in any institution' (p. 384).

• *Passion* Welch argues for organisations which 'ignite passion', and leaders at all levels who care passionately for the role they are undertaking and the people they are working with and for.

• *Stretch* Reaching out for aspirations.

• *Celebrations* Jack Welch shares with his British counterpart, Sir John Harvey-Jones, a belief that success has to be celebrated to keep motivation going and people stretching.

• *Aligning rewards with measurements* Setting and measuring the right objectives.

• *Differentiation develops great organisations* This is a tough one, especially in public sector organisations, where the rewards and incentives are less, but it is true to say that the leader who listens carefully to staff on the front line will often hear them being the most critical of staff who don't perform – for precisely the reason that they have to carry the performance gap that is left.

• *Owning the people* One of Welch's mottos was: '

You own the businesses. You're renting the people.

• *Appraisals all the time.*

• *Culture counts* Welch is critical of a number of major companies who merged and didn't sort out the issue of culture. This is the same in any type of company, any size, private or public. You must have a positive culture and you cannot have multiple cultures.

• *Strategy* In Welch's opinion: 'business success is less a function of grandiose predictions than it is a result of being able to respond rapidly to real changes as they occur. That's why strategy has to be dynamic and anticipatory' (p. 390). Compare this with Rommel's opinion that: 'no plan survives contact' (Fraser, 1994, p. 418) and Shackleton's approach where his strategy was underpinned by a range of flexible alternatives (see Morrell and Capparell, 2001).

• *Competitors* Never underestimate them.

• *The field* Welch spent at least a third of his time with the GE business out in he field. As he puts it: 'I always reminded myself: headquarters doesn't make anything or sell anything. Banging around the field was my best shot of getting some idea about what was really going on' (p. 391).

• *Initiatives versus tactics* In 20 years, GE had only four major initiatives – Globalisation, Services, Six SIGMA and E-business. These initiatives are designed to create fundamental change. Tactical moves are also important, but it is vital to understand the difference.

• *The communicator* Welch describes himself as 'an outrageous champion of everything we did'. He believed it was most important to have a fundamental sense of the values and mission of the organisation and keep repeating that time and time again so that people lived and breathed it.

• *Employee feedback* GE concentrated on fundamental issues around the theme: 'Is the company you read about in the annual report, the company you work for?' (p. 393).

• *The advertising manager* Welch saw the Chief Executive's role as being involved in something that many people would see as a detail, something to be delegated or something to be passed on to experts. Welch believed that the image of the company was something that he needed to be personally involved in: 'Image mattered. I was convinced it was my job' (p. 395).

• *Managing loose, managing tight* 'A lot of this is pure instinct. I managed tight when I sensed I could make a difference. I managed loose when I knew I had little if anything to offer' (p. 395).

• *Your backroom is somebody else's front room* This is a bit like Peters and Waterman's (1982) idea of 'Stick to the Knitting'. Basically, each organisation should do what they need to do and concentrate on that.

• *Speed and size* Welch advocates taking decisions quickly and keeping an eye on the size of the organisation – using size when the organisation needs weight behind it, and breaking parts of the organisation down into smaller discrete teams and units to re-energise.

Bennis, W. (1989) *On Becoming a Leader*, New York, NY: Addison-Wesley.
Fraser, D. (1994) *Nights Cross: A Life of Field Marshall Erwin Rommel*, London: HarperCollins.
Keegan, J. (1987) *The Mask of Command*, New York, NY: Viking Penguin.
Morrell, M. and Capparell, S. (2001) *Shackleton's Way: Leadership Lessons From The Great Antartic Explorer*, London: Nicholas Brealey.
Peters, T. and Waterman, R. (1982) *In Search of Excellence: Lessons from America's Best-run Companies*, New York, NY: HarperCollins.
Welch, J. with Byrne, J. (2001) *Jack: What I've Learned Leading a Great Company and Great People*, London: Headline Press.

Cardinal Basil Hume (1923-1999) – Spiritual Leader

The rule of St Benedict, written in the 6th century for communities attempting to light a beacon of civilisation to illuminate the 'Dark Ages' with love and learning, has recently come back into focus as a way of studying community leadership and living and achieving a sense of balance at a time of societal and personal stresses.

Reading the Rule (Benedict of Nursia, circa 540 AD) there are lessons for modern leaders in ethical governance. For instance, in Chapter 2 on the 'Qualities of the Abbot' (the monastic community's Chief Executive), St Benedict states: '

> To be worthy of the task of governing a monastery, the Abbot must always remember what his title signifies and act as a superior should' (Chapter 2, verse 1).

And again:

> The Abbot must always remember what he is and remember what he is called, aware that more will be expected of a man to whom more has been entrusted' (Chapter 2, verse 30).

Governance is set in the context of stewardship so that:

> Once in office, the Abbot must keep constantly in mind the nature of the burden he has received, and remember to whom he will have to give an account of his stewardship (Luke 16: 2). Let him recognise that his goal must be profit for the monks, not pre-eminence for himself. He ought, therefore, to be learned ..., so that he has a treasury of knowledge from which he can bring out what is new and – what is old. (Chapter 64, verses 7-9 inclusive)

Ambition for oneself is not encouraged. Benedict describes the personality too often seen in authority: 'Excitable, anxious, extreme, obstinate, jealous or over suspicious he must not be. Such a man is never at rest'. On the contrary, 'he must so arrange everything that the strong have something to yearn for and the weak nothing to run from' (Chapter 64, verses 16 and 19).

Hume was headmaster of a Benedictine school and Abbot of Ampleforth before becoming Cardinal Archbishop of Westminster in 1976. As one of his obituarists wrote: 'The monk lived on in the Cardinal' (Hebblethwaite, 1999).

As befits the spiritual leader of a faith that believes in a transcendent being, Hume always impressed people he met as someone who connected both vertically and with those around him.

When John Crowley, Bishop of Middlesbrough, delivered the funeral homily on Hume, he declared:

For thirty-five years as a monk and for twenty-three years as Archbishop, Cardinal Hume centred himself on God. And from that store of wisdom he fed us. He addressed head-on the God-shaped emptiness which is within everyone. Without ever seeking it, he became a reassuring light for perhaps millions of people in this country and beyond. (*The Tablet*, 3 July 1999)

To talk about 'God' in a secular society is somewhat uncomfortable, but there is no doubt that this is an age when the search for some kind of 'spirituality' is a pilgrimage which many people embark on. Rolheiser (1998) writes of:

> An unquenchable fire, a restlessness, a longing, a disquiet, an appetitiveness, a loneliness, a gnawing nostalgia, a wildness that cannot be tamed, a congenital all-embracing ache that lies at the centre of human experience and is the ultimate force that drives everything else. This dis-ease is universal. Desire gives no exemptions. (p. 4)

Rolheiser goes on to say that:

> Spirituality is, ultimately, about what we do with that desire. What we do with our longings, both in terms of handling the pain and the hope that they bring us, is our spirituality. Thus, when Plato says that we are on fire because our souls come from beyond and that beyond is, through the longing and hope that its fire creates in us, trying to draw us back towards itself, he is laying out the broad outlines for a spirituality. (p. 5)

It was this disease which Basil Hume sought to identify, address and provide some consolation and answers for, which was the reason why he drew unto himself many people outside his own faith, or with no formal faith at all.

Allied to this vertical integration between human beings and the Other, Hume had an ability to relate to a wide range of people. John Crowley thought that this was partly because: 'that sense of the worth of the Other is strongly influenced by his conviction that every human being he meets is superior to him in some way' (Butler, 1999, p. 31).

Father Luke Jolly, Co-ordinator of the Centre for Spirituality at Worth Abbey in Sussex, was amazed to bump into Cardinal Hume in London some years ago, and find that Hume knew exactly who he was, though they'd never met before.

Hume's connectedness with a range of people from different cultures may have partly stemmed from his birth to an agnostic Scottish heart surgeon and a French mother. He had a good command of a number of European languages, and unusually in an English Archbishop led the convocation of European Catholic Bishops. The European and world dimensions are very evident from the contributors to Carolyn Butler's book (Butler, 1999) and there are contributions from Lord Jakobovitz, Sheikh Zaki Badawi and Cardinal Carlo Maria Martini.

In terms of his leadership, Hume was essentially an inclusive leader within an autocratic structure. The General Secretary to the Bishop's Conference recalls that his style of being chair promoted the 'discovery of the common mind'. Minority voices were always given a chance to speak, and a great deal of trouble was taken by Hume to discern the best direction before acting. Sometimes he was criticised for being too cautious, but he would often work deftly behind the scenes to produce change, and would attempt to find and steer a middle course between two extremes if that was right. Julian Filochowski, Director of CAFOD, recalled, in a conversation with Peter Gilbert that it was Hume who was the only one to persuade Prime Minister Callaghan not to sell arms to a South American government which would have been used to oppress the civilian population. In 1996, the Catholic Church published 'The Common Good', a document on ethical, social issues, which true to the spirit of the rule of St Benedict, looked back to the creative route of the past and forward into the future.

Cardinal Hume allied a sense of humour to a deep seriousness and dignity. Clifford Longley, a prominent Catholic commentator and journalist, wrote of Hume's significance:

> Maybe the main part of it, was to be at the level of public image and perception rather than at the level of policy or strategy. That does not reduce its importance. Image and perception play a crucial role in chasing the relationship between a large historical organisation like the Catholic Church and the society within which it has to operate. (quoted in Butler, p. 92)

Cardinal Martini has pointed out that at a time when people demonstrate 'a great hunger for spirituality', a spiritual leader who 'embodies the long tradition of prayer of the Benedictine', and who is also able to speak to the concerns of present-day society, has much to offer (Butler, 1999, p. 78).

Timothy Radcliffe, a theologian, in talking of Hume, quotes the 14th century mystic, Meister Eckhart, who wrote:

> People should not worry so much about what they should do; rather about what they should be. If we and our ways are good, then what we do will be highly valued. (cited in Butler, 1999, p. 53, see also Charles, 2009)

Benedict of Nursia (circa 540 AD), 'The Rule of St Benedict' in Fry, T. (ed.) (1982).
Butler, C. (ed.) (1999) *Basil Hume: By His Friends*, London: HarperCollins.
Catholic Bishops' Conference of England and Wales (1996) *The Common Good and the Catholic Church's Social Teaching*, London: CBCEW.
Hebblethwaite, P. (1999) 'Obituary on Cardinal Hume', *The Guardian*, 18 June.
Rolheiser, R. (1998) *Seeking Spirituality*, London: Hodder and Stoughton.

Dame Cicely Saunders – Founder of the Hospice Movement (1918-2005)

> I have seen people in Japan, New Zealand, in Australia, South Africa, Zimbabwe, Bermuda, all over the United States and all over Europe, who regard Cicely as their teacher, the person who originated all that they are doing.
>
> (Richard Lamerton, Cicely Saunders' first houseman at St Christopher's Hospice, quoted in du Boulay, 1984, p. 231)

The extent of Cicely Saunders' work in founding the modern hospice movement was well outlined by Dr Lamerton in 1984, and by now is far more extensive. The depth of her contribution is described by the biographer herself:

> Cicely has transformed the face of death throughout the world... she has brought about this revolution by the effective use of drugs and by changing attitudes to the one certainty of life and its greatest mystery. *Through her, dying has lost something of its sting.* (du Boulay, 1984, p. 231 – emphasis added)

Most people are afraid of the pain involved in a terminal disease, the possibilities of dying lonely and afraid, and what, if anything, lies on the other side of the 'curtain'.

One of the greatest services we can do for people individually is to ease that passage through pain relief, hope and companionship. Dame Cicely Saunders, with her very unusual training in social work, nursing and then medicine, allied to great determination and a strong vision, has given much hope to so many people.

There is perhaps the danger in being too psychological when considering the achievements of leaders, but very contented people from entirely happy childhoods don't always have the 'itch' to achieve which drives many acknowledged leadership figures. Certainly Cicely Saunders had a less than perfect childhood, caught between her warm, energetic, somewhat overbearing father and her mother who had great difficulty in expressing affection. Saunders was really mothered at an early age by one of her father's relatives, but aunt Daisy was sent away when it was clear that the baby preferred her to Saunders' mother.

Du Boulay remarks that the inability to love her mother created considerable guilt in the young Saunders, and one can speculate as to whether her love for two terminally ill men, David Tasma and Antoni Michniewicz, were aspects of distrust for long-term relationships?

At school, her headmistress wrote of her: 'Although not a natural leader, she has been a good Head of House' (du Boulay, 1984, p. 23). Interestingly, the young woman felt that she had learned something very specific – a feeling for the underdog, 'because I felt I'd been an underdog fairly frequently myself' (quoted in du Boulay, p. 23).

But, despite a rather average school achievement, her biographer identifies a number of her father's characteristics that were already beginning to become evident: his ability and energy, the breadth of his interests, and 'his powers of leadership'. She said of him: 'All my father's geese were swans, he was marvellous at inspiring people' (p. 28). This was certainly said of her although, as her biographer points out, she was not always an easy person to work for and with.

Moving from school to St. Anne's College, Oxford, she studied under Ms C.V. Butler, the economics tutor of whom du Boulay writes that she 'had such influence over generations of social workers between 1914 and 1945' (p. 31). But Cicely Saunders left before completing a degree; the advent of the second world war attracting her to undertake nurse training. There is an interesting link here with the life of Florence Nightingale, as it was to the Nightingale Training School that Saunders went, and it was very much the Nightingale standards with which she was imbued. Her years at nurse training are again a good antidote to those who believe that leaders spring fully armed like Athena from the forehead of Zeus! The nursing supervisory reports describe her as diffident and 'somewhat handicapped by nervousness', with what appeared to be 'an inferiority complex' (p. 35). Some of the remarks seem to describe some attributes of Saunders' mother, but other reports remark on the description 'determined' also appears and the reference from her headmistress to St Thomas's Hospital Nursing School states: 'she has always given serious thoughts to her career, and I should be greatly surprised if anything deterred her once she had decided to embark on a piece of work' (p. 25).

One other neat connection with Florence Nightingale, and a neat description of Saunders' sense of humour and willingness to depart from conventional paths, is the skit about Florence Nightingale which she put on at the end of year party. Summoned to Matron, Saunders was told in round terms:

> You'll never be a good nurse, nurse, if you do not learn there are some things about which one does not make jokes. If you are really thinking of being a Nightingale Nurse, you must not make jokes about Miss Nightingale! (p. 37)

Plagued by severe back trouble, Saunders completed her training, but was advised not to work as a nurse. Instead, she became an almoner, the role which turned into medical social work in the mid 1950s. Inevitably, du Boulay's biography of Cicely Saunders has quite a focus on her Christian beliefs. Suffice it to say that this spiritual dimension was very much part of her vision for a specific service which catered for the physical and spiritual needs of people who were dying and their families.

Saunders' love for David Tasma, a patient from the Warsaw ghetto, who was dying of inoperable cancer; their discussions about care for the dying; and the gift in his will of £500 for her – 'I'll be a window in your home' (quoted in du Boulay, p. 58); coupled with her next job at St Luke's Home for the Dying, proved to be important drivers towards her ultimate goal. It was one of the doctors that she worked with who said to her: 'Go and read medicine, it's the doctors who desert the dying' (quoted in du Boulay, p. 63).

Qualifying as a doctor, Cicely became involved with St Joseph's Hospice in Hackney, where nursing care was superb, but pain control was elementary. Saunders' work gave patients the ability to be free of pain without being comatose. A group of social work students went around St Joseph's, following Dr Saunders' involvement and made the following observations:

- An absence of pain and drowsiness.

- Liveliness and peacefulness.

- An indefinable atmosphere which left one feeling that death was nothing to be worried about – a sort of homecoming.

- Integration – patients, staff and visitors were all of equal importance; there seemed to be no dividing barriers. We noticed especially how easy it was to talk to patients and how easily they accepted us.

- Simplicity of approach to the problem of pain.

- People are helped to come to terms with death in a way that suits them best as individuals. (du Boulay, p. 72)

From her unique perspective of being almost a multidisciplinary team of her own, Cicely Saunders was able to observe that for the majority of doctors, death was seen as a defeat, a failure which needed to be avoided or to go unacknowledged. Saunders was determined to found her own hospice, based on her unique approach, and set out her vision and the practical steps in two short, clear documents: 'The Need' and 'The Scheme'. As her biographer remarks: 'Her distilled experience was committed to eight pages of closely typed confident prose' (du Boulay, p. 86). Although a supporter of the National Health Service, Saunders wanted her hospice to be independent so there could freedom of thought and action, but good relations were needed, she foresaw, with the commissioning health authorities and the local community.

Aware that the Ministry of Health might see her scheme as a criticism of current services, and therefore block it, Saunders worked very tactfully and persuasively with senior national and local managers; she also used her powers of persuasion with charitable foundations and local planning committees to fund and build St Christopher's.

In leadership terms, she had the difficult task of acting as a founder and medical director, and in a sense as 'a benevolent despot', (du Boulay, p. 101); but at the same time, building a 'community', one without a religious rule (such as the rule of St Benedict), but a large team where people have to work together for the common good. Clearly, Saunders was not always an easy person to work with and for. She had an incredible knack of listening to patients and carers: 'An almost uncanny capacity for really listening and enabling people to speak of their deep inner pain' (du Boulay, p. 141).

Du Boulay remarks that perhaps part of her secret lies in an Hasidic question and answer she often recalls:

> Why do you say you should listen to someone as if you were looking on water rather than as if you were looking on a mirror? Because you have to be very still if you are going to see in water, you can so easily disturb it.

On the other hand, colleagues sometimes felt that she wasn't always as careful of them as she was of her patients. That demand for high standards could sometimes come at a cost, though as one nurse wrote: 'How can one express in words the quiet, endless learning here?' (du Boulay, p. 147).

As well as leading on hospice care in the UK, Cicely Saunders had an immense effect overseas. She made an immediate impact when she went over to the United States, and Dr Klagsbrun, Clinical Professor of Psychiatry at Columbia University, described her as follows:

> Dr Saunders is strong, courageous and persistent - some might even consider her stubborn. She is articulate and has a basic faith and trust in her message. She is relentless in pursuing her goals and is quite unconcerned with the opinion of others, if these opinions jeopardise her work. She evinces humour, and a sharp wit when it is needed. These characteristics have been crucial in the establishment of St Christopher's Hospice; yet Dr Saunders has never acknowledged the importance of her personality, or the impact of her leadership, in the field of medical care for patients facing death. (quoted in du Boulay, p. 149).

Du Boulay, S. (1984) *Cicely Saunders: The Founder of the Modern Hospice Movement*, London: Hodder and Stoughton.

STEP factors

- Sociological

- Technological

- Economic

- Political

SWOT analysis

STRENGTHS   WEAKNESSES

OPPORTUNITIES   THREATS

Images of leadership

- Images

- Words

- Concepts

(Source: Blanchard et al., 1996)

Styles of leadership

- **Supporting**

  High supportive

  Low directive

- **Coaching**

  High directive

  High supportive

Styles of leadership (cont)

- **Delegating**

  Low supportive

  Low directive

- **Directing**

  High directive

  Low supportive

(Source: Blanchard et al., 1986)

Theories X, Y and Z

- **Theory X**

  People dislike work and try to avoid it

- **Theory Y**

  People see work as fulfilling part of their psychological need to find value and meaning

• **Theory Z**

People identify with a corporate vision, value system and presentation which is accurate and explicit

(Sources: McGregor, 1960 and Gilbert, 2005, p. 63)

Origin of terms

Leadership

From the old English word, 'Laedan': a road, a way, the path of a ship at sea. Related to another old English word 'Lithan' – 'to travel'. A leader is a person who discovers the right direction in which to travel; takes other people with them; guides them and supports them on the journey; and keeps the goal always in their mind's eye.

(Sources: Adair, 2002 and Gilbert, 2005)

Origin of terms (cont)

Management

Stems from two words: Latin noun 'manus' – a hand – and its derivative, the Italian verb 'maneggiare' – to handle or train.

(Sources: Adair, 2002 and Gilbert, 2005)

Leadership vs Management

Managers	**Leaders**
Focus on systems and structure	Focus on people
Maintain	Develop
Ask how and when	Ask what and why
Concentrate on planning and budgeting	Set a direction and align people
Have their eye on the bottom line	Have their eye on the horizon
Are deductive and rational	Are inductive and intuitive

Leadership vs Management (cont)

Managers	**Leaders**
Ensure the accomp-lishment of plans by controlling and problem-solving	Achieve goals through motivating and inspiring people
Cope with current complexity	Cope with change
Do things right	Do the right thing

(Adapted from Kotter, 1990)

Adair's three functions

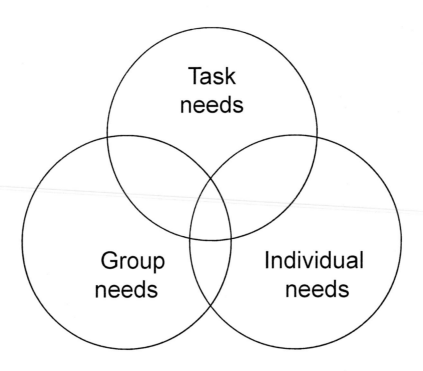

(Source: Adair, 1983)

Task functions

- Defining the task

- Making a plan

- Allocating work and resources

- Controlling quality and tempo of work

- Checking performance against the plan

- Adjusting the plan

Individual functions

- Attending to personal problems

- Praising individuals

- Giving status

- Recognising and using individual abilities

- Training the individual

Group functions

- Setting standards

- Maintaining discipline

- Building team spirit

- Encouraging, motivating, giving a sense of purpose

- Appointing sub-leaders

- Ensuring communication within the group

- Training the group

(Source: Adair, 1983)

Flamholtz and Randall

Playing the 'inner game of management' successfully

• Being able to manage your own self-esteem so that you derive satisfaction from the things managers are sup-posed to do

• Being able to manage your need for direct control over people and results

• Being able to manage your need to be liked so that it does not interfere with per-forming the managerial role

(Source: Flamholtz, E. and Randall, Y., 1989)

Self and others

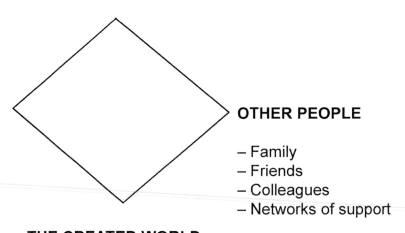

THE OTHER

– God
– Philosophy
– Belief Systems

SELF

– Self awareness
– Being grounded in
core values
– Becoming a more
effective person/leader

OTHER PEOPLE

– Family
– Friends
– Colleagues
– Networks of support

THE CREATED WORLD

– Landscape
– Seascape
– The Animal
– Minerals, plants and so on

The diamond of self and others (Gilbert, 2005, p13)

Five areas of need and development

- Social and emotional

- Mental or cognitive

- Spiritual

- Physical

- Creative

(Source: Gilbert, 2002)

Electronic supply of the worksheets, biographies and presentation slides from *Devoloping Leadership*

If you would like to receive a PDF and Powerpoint of the worksheets, biographies and presentation slides from this manual, please complete the form on the facing page, tear out this page, and return it to us. Please note that photocopies are not acceptable, nor are applications made through e-mail, phone or fax.

Please keep a copy of the completed form for your own records.

This PDF is free.

Please note

RHP reserves the right to withdraw this offer at any time without any prior notice.

RHP reserves the right to qualify or reject any application which it is not completely satisfied is on an original torn-out page from the back of a purchased manual.

Terms and conditions for use of the worksheets, biographies and presentation slides from *Developing Leadership*

1. Buying a copy of *Developing Leadership* and completing this form gives the individual who signs the form permission to use the materials in the PDF and Powerpoint that will be sent from RHP for their own use only.

2. The hard copies that they then print from the PDF are subject to the same permissions and restrictions that are set out in the 'photocopying permission' section at the front of this manual. (See page xi.)

3. Under no circumstances should they forward or copy the electronic materials to anyone else.

4. If the person who signs this form wants a licence to be granted for wider use of the electronic materials within their organisation, network or client base, they must make a request directly to RHP fully detailing the proposed use. All requests will be reviewed on their own merits.

   • If the request is made when submitting this form to RHP, the request should be made in writing and should accompany this form.

   • If the request is made later, it should be made in an email sent to help@russelhouse.co.uk, and should not only fully detail the proposed use, but also give the details of the person whose name and contact details were on the original application form.

RHP and the authors expect this honour system to be followed respectfully, by individuals and organisations whom we in turn respect. RHP will act to protect authors' copyright if they become aware of it being infringed.

I would like to receive a free PDF and Powerpoint of the worksheets, biographies and presentation slides from *Developing Leadership*

*Name _____

*Address _____

_____

_____

_____

*Post code _____

*Contact phone number _____

*e-mail address _____ (to which the PDF and Powerpoint will be e-mailed)

I have read, and accept, the terms and conditions on the facing page. I understand that RHP may use this information to contact me about other matters and publications, but that RHP will not make my details available to any other organisations.

*Signed _____   *Date _____

* All sections marked with an asterisk **must be completed**, or the form will be returned to the postal address given here.

Please return to:
Russell House Publishing
4 St George's House
Uplyme Rd
Lyme Regis
Dorset
DT7 3LS

Learning for Practice

This manual is one of a series of learning and development resources to be published by Russell House Publishing under the guidance of series editor Neil Thompson. Each manual will offer invaluable support and guidance for training and development staff in organisations; lecturers and tutors in colleges and universities; and managers keen to play an active role in promoting learning within their team or staff group.

Other titles already published or confirmed for publication include:

• **Meaning and values** By Bernard Moss and Neil Thompson

Drawing on three books in the Theory into Practice series (*Values* and *Religion and Spirituality* by Bernard Moss and *Power and Empowerment* by Neil Thompson) this learning resource manual offers important guidance for people delivering training and development for staff across the helping professions who are committed to promoting best practice.

978-1-905541-31-7. 2008

• **Working with adults** By Jackie Martin and Sue Thompson

Drawing on three books in the *Theory into Practice* series (*Safeguarding Adults* by Jackie Martin; *Age Discrimination* by Sue Thompson; and *Community Care* by Neil Thompson and Sue Thompson), this learning resource manual offers important guidance for people delivering training and development for staff across the helping professions involved in supporting adults.

978-1-905541-39-3. 2008

• **Tackling bullying and harassment in the workplace** By Neil Thompson

Sadly, bullying and harassment are far more prevalent in organisations than most people realise. This learning resource will be an excellent guide for anyone involved in delivering training and development for staff and managers across the whole range of 'people professions'.

978-1-905541-44-7. 2009

• **Promoting equality, valuing diversity** By Neil Thompson

Neil Thompson's work on anti-discriminatory practice has become very highly respected for its clarity, successfully combining theoretical depth with practical usefulness. Building on his success in this area, this manual will provide a range of exercises carefully designed to enable participants to maximise their learning about these complex and challenging issues.

978-1-905541-49-2. 2009

Responding to loss By Bernard Moss

Loss and grief can affect anyone in any organisation. For some staff, managers and leaders, dealing with them is a frequent experience because of the nature of their work. For others, it may be less frequent; but they are still somehow expected to know what to do when a death or other loss does occur – even if no-one has actually helped them learn.

For any trainer – with or without previous experience in this area – it offers:

- a foundation for developing understanding of how grief and loss affect people, groups, teams and organisations; and how staff can remain effective while also being dignified and sensitive
- advice on how increasing awareness and understanding can be of value to the people you work with and to your organisation
- help and guidance on delivering training on this with confidence
- 18 exercises, 12 copiable worksheets, and presentation slides, from which you can pick and choose to deliver your training
- the opportunity to obtain the worksheets, presentation slides and case study in electronic format – free of charge – directly from RHP after you have purchased the manual.

978-1-905541-58-4. 2010

Supervision skills By Neil Thompson and Peter Gilbert

Getting the best out of staff owes so much to the skill and commitment of the supervisor. An effective supervisor is able to create win-win situations where everybody is happy: the employee fulfils their potential; the employers get the best return on their investment; and people who use the organisation's services benefit from the quality of the staff member's practice.

This important manual in the *Learning for Practice* series shows that supervision is not simply a matter of making sure the supervisee is doing their job properly. It also involves helping staff achieve the best quality of work that they are capable of by maximising learning, promoting high levels of well-being and addressing any conflicts, tensions of other obstacles to optimal practice.

The manual provides background information about the role and significance of supervision and a set of learning exercises carefully designed to promote professional development. Anyone interested in promoting learning about supervision skills will find much of interest and use in this clear and well-written set of resources. Effective supervision is an important foundation of good practice, and this manual provides a sound foundation for helping supervisors develop the skills they need to do their job to the best of their ability.

978-1-905541-62-1. Due 2010

Further manuals are planned. Details will be available at www.russellhouse.co.uk

Books by Neil Thompson: A selection

Published by Russell House

Power and empowerment By Neil Thompson

Empowerment has become a well-used term across a wide variety of work settings that involve dealing with people and their problems. And what of power? It is a central theme of human services practice but, like empowerment, is often only loosely examined. "A useful gateway to the complexity of power and empowerment... It is a book which speaks a strong commitment to social justice... Neil Thompson provides an altogether more subtle and compelling analysis... I can see experienced practitioners and practice teachers enjoying it. This is a book that goes well beyond the rhetoric." Professor Mark Doel, Sheffield Hallam University.   978-1-903855-99-7. 2007

Community care By Neil Thompson and Sue Thompson

"A thoughtful and critical account of underpinning theory and practice issues." Community Care. "Emphasises the importance of a critical approach to reflective and systematic practice." Professional Social Work. "An admirably accessible text... skillfully designed to build up readers' knowledge and understanding by introducing key themes and their interrelationships before systematically relating them to practice" Community Safety Journal.   978-1-903855-58-4. 2005

Published by Palgrave Macmillan

People problems By Neil Thompson

A companion volume to the best-selling text, *People Skills*, this important book offers helpful guidance on problem-solving approaches and includes details of 50 problem solving tools – some long-established and well proven and some new and innovative methods. An excellent guide for anyone involved in the 'people professions' charged with helping people address their problems.   978-1-403943-04-0. 2006

The critically reflective practitioner By Sue Thompson and Neil Thompson

Reflective practice is increasingly being recognised as a necessary foundation for well informed professional practice. This book explores what is involved in the theory and practice of adopting not only a reflective approach in general, but specifically a critically reflective approach. The implications of adopting a critically reflective approach are drawn out so that students, practitioners, managers and educators can all have a clearer picture of why critically reflective practice should be seen as an essential basis for high-quality practice.   978-0-230573-18-5. 2008

The social work companion By Neil Thompson and Sue Thompson

This major text offers a compendium of information to act as a basis for developing the knowledge, skills and values needed to become a qualified social worker. This is an essential text for all social work students and practice teachers that will also be of value and interest to established practitioners and managers who are keen to revisit their roots from time to time. Having quickly established itself as a bestseller, this book will no doubt prove to be a standard text for many years to come.

978-1-403937-957. 2008

Books by Peter Gilbert: A selection

Leadership: Being effective and remaining human By Peter Gilbert

"Asserts a powerful and clear image of the human services leader." The International Journal of Leadership in Public Service

"Reminds us that leadership occurs at all levels... impressive." Nursing Standard

"The chapter on the use – and potential abuse – of personal power and authority is essential reading... suitable for anyone practicing leadership at whatever level and provides excellent scope for reflection on personal aspirations and performance." Social Caring

"An immense amount of useful material." Youth & Policy

978-1-903855-76-8. 2005

Social work and mental health: The value of everything By Peter Gilbert with Peter Bates, Sarah Carr, Michael Clark, Nick Gould and Greg Slay

"Elegantly written and logically presented... essential reading for all those embarking on social work careers, those who are already qualified and particularly for commissioners and managers of services. I found the book educational and informative and I would strongly recommend it to others."

From a pre-publication review by Neil Carr OBE, South Staffordshire and Shropshire Healthcare NHS Foundation Trust

This new edition of Peter Gilbert's *The Value of Everything: Social Work and its Importance in the Field of Mental Health* (RHP, 2003) maintains the focus on the values that social work espouses as a profession, and its value in current mental health services. New chapters have been added around:

• social inclusion
• personalisation
• research
• spirituality
• the role of the social worker following new mental health legislation in 2005 and 2007
• an overview of policy up to the current time.

With mental health increasingly being recognised as crucial for a healthy and productive nation, and a vital component in the regeneration of communities, the current reality and future possibilities for social work in mental health services are becoming clearer.

This book:

• celebrates and promotes multi-disciplinary work and the integration of perspectives
• sets social work as a major contributor to a truly whole-person and whole-systems approach to mental health.

- values those who use mental health services as people with their own unique strengths, needs and experiences
- addresses issues of identity and equality
- provides clear theoretical frameworks for understanding barriers to developing those relationships that enable social workers to recognise the capacities of service users
- discusses the merits of different models for understanding and working with mental or emotional distress
- uses research and ideas drawn from sociology, psychiatry, psychology and even economics to emphasise how social work is able to utilise the best of everything that is available for the service users' and carers' benefit.

Timely, it considers the value of social work in light of what users and carers want from services; the value base of the new policies of reform; the role of the social worker in different settings; and ways of taking values and skills into these new settings.

It will boost the confidence of social workers by reinforcing the tremendous resource that they are to people in the greatest need in our society; and will help partner professions and agencies value the contribution that social work can bring.

"A fresh perspective on just what is possible... We are challenged to make real the proposition that 'mental health is everyone's business'... This is a book full of insights... It is challenging, it is inspiring and at the same time, it is a really good read."

From a pre-publication review by Professor Christine King, Vice Chancellor, Staffordshire University

978-1-905541-60-7. 2010